Hastings Street

A Story of a Converted Man

Yongjea John Han

ISBN-13: 978-1-7750387-7-1

CONTENTS

Chapter 1

ON THE STREETS of Hastings, winter comes early; I already feel a chill coming up from the bottom at night. At the end of last summer, if it was not for a winter coat that was provided by a charitable organization, it would not have the capacity to fight a frightening cold air.

The leaves of the trees on the street were already yellow, and the warm sunlight of the day was appreciative. Winds blowing through this high-street building can always predict where that direction will go. This is also the place that does not change that much.

The routine here begins with asking each other questions about what happened last night.

People are predicting everything that can happen to anyone who is caught up in a police station during the night and even in the cold winter, stories of strangers who occasionally fall asleep on the road and die. Perhaps it was a story that would not fit into reality for people with ordinary homes and families.

A place where they can not get out of here easily when they step on foot, the heat of summer or the cold of winter do not let them get out of here.

Some are already living here on the streets for over five years. His name was Jim, and the rumor that I heard was that I did not know anything about him, nor did they want to know about him, except that he came to Vancouver to escape the cold of Nova Scotia. One obvious fact is that when I first met him on the street, his appearance changed a lot.

It was never a good meaning. His face was getting older because that he spent most of his money on drugs and alcohol with a little more than $200 a month from the government. The actual age was around 25, but his appearance was already in his mid-40s. I have not been able to get out of the same routine everyday with them. It was a big shackle and chain to Jim or me.

Jim and I did not get so deep together. He was already drug addicted enough to live an abnormal life. I remember that I had a real conversation with him only once or twice. Everyone living here is barely holding onto the day with a story like Jim. Everyone will have a clear reason for life. I can not meet him here now. The rumor was heard that he went into a recovery center with an overdose of medication and moved to another area with other friends he met on the street and was living there constantly. There are not only homeless people here on the streets of Hastings in Vancouver. In every city in Canada, homeless people and the poor life are there. This is not just Canada. Perhaps the city where all the people of the world live has the lowest class of society like us. Maybe it is true that civilization calls for another poverty.

It seems that richness necessarily includes the sacrifice of the poor. When I look at this city, I think. People living on the streets are socially weak. If they had the will to live independently, they would not have been homeless. There is always the danger that the body alone can not bear looking at those who are weak, mentally and physically ill have become extremely natural here.

Sometimes I think of a corn field that grows in a wide field on the outskirts of Vancouver. I think the city resembles the corn field a lot. The field of corn is so wide that it is not easy to return to its original position once it gets lost in it. The maize stand is spread like a labyrinth.

A lot of corn can grow and come to harvest quickly. This is the city. The people who walked the streets, the beggars, and their gaze looking at them begging for a little favor resembled the corn in the labyrinth. Is it the craziness of a soul that is not always filled? Their hearts seemed to have too many gaps that were not filled. Above all, they did not reap in the harvest season and left them in the field, so their crops became so raw that they could not be eaten later. People in the blind spots of society that no one ever looked at, it were the abandoned fields that missed the harvest time. The greetings among the people who passed by here were simple, with only a rough list of words made in their language.

"Hey, where have you been last night?"

A normal person has a house and a family. But the greetings with them were all related to the survival. They had to survive during their nights on the street.

And it is just about some information concerning a free lunch area where you can go and live in a different world than ordinary people, for example, having spent a lot of money on living expenses, and now they grumbled having to spend the next pay day with no money left.

Returning to the corn story again, it is true that not all corn is full. The sunlight and the weather of the year are good when considering all things well, and the life here is the same as it is when some year's empty corn has and the fields are not growing. It is the appearance of them but empty. It is true that they are not full, their hearts are divided, and they are torn by wounds, bearing all their pain and sorrow in their hearts.

Every year, the world is ranked as the best place to live. Vancouver Canada is one of the most livable cities of the year. I am now living in Hastings Street, close to downtown Vancouver.

Even those who live on this street have a heart that is hurt and has a story, but if they can find one thing in common, there is a great sense of pride in Canada. They are proud of the fact that they are Canadians.

Their wounds are extremely personal. Healing for the wound is necessary but more important than where they are living now.

Vancouver seems to have some amazing power to make people.

Compared to the volatile Canadian weather, the weather here in Vancouver is relatively mild. There is hardly anything down to zero in the middle of the winter. And the temperature does not raise that much in the summer. However, from September when the rainy season begins, there are more rainy days. During that period, cold weather is transmitted to the human bone even if it is not cold in the middle of the winter. People on the streets avoid the cold as much as they spend the night in sheltered areas.

As cold as their wounds, the cold makes them

lonelier and depresses people as much as the pressure of low pressure to push their hearts down. Many people on the streets have a lot of illnesses with such serious depression or mental disabilities. They are easily exposed to drugs become addicted and insecure to live almost every day. Variable weather has a profound effect on people's minds. It works as if it were an earthquake with little notice. Before a major earthquake, there is a precursor phenomenon. Prepare for an earthquake in advance.

Such is the fluctuation of microscopic land or the change of emotions of animals.
Vancouver is not a safe zone from earthquakes. The neighborhood is called Vancouver Island. It is the beautiful island where the government of British Columbia starts for the first time.

However, in the nearby sea, frequent earthquakes begin to take place deep in the sea. The aftermath of this happened long ago in Vancouver.

Frequent weather changes the minds of people. Especially during the rainy season, this place is close to the Pacific Ocean and it often rains and even gets cold. Then the mind of the person changes to that. Sometimes it has a clear day for a few months but their mind is always depressed with the rainy weather that continues.

In particular, people living on the streets feel more depressed by cold and loneliness. There are volunteers who come from time to time, but some refuse even this help. In the end, they end up lonely life on the street.

By last winter I still remember that time. I do not know his name, but for a while, I can not see his face and asked his friend where he is. But the answer is that he slept in the street at night and died of the frozen. In the place where he was about to escape from the cold, he was drunk and he fell asleep to death. Of course, he also had severe depression and mental illness. Every time I hear such news, people here are as frightened as they look. They say like that:

"I do not have anything to do with me, I just want to survive." The thought about the death of others also reacts casually. I just have to survive, how I am worried about others. Only the self is interested in survival. This is so much like a jungle or grassland. Where the weak can not survive, the streets are maintained by those who are.

It is the saddest, lonely and cruel reality in some way. It is a street where there is missing for more humanity, and it is a place to miss a person. There is a philosophy there.

"Do not ask for anything if you do not ask anything."It is because there are many people who are caught up in the past. And it has a lot of secrets that can not be known to others. People living on this street are lonely.

Even though they are talking together, their conversation is full of loneliness. They want to talk, but they want to be comforted to each other. In that world, they continue their lives with their own principles and survival methods. An indifferent attitude is an expression of interest that can best be shown to them. There are a lot of words in their mouths mixed with truth and exaggeration.

So indifferent expression is the greatest defense to avoid unnecessary controversy and contention. I was able to grasp some of the techniques of conversation here by seeing some people fighting each other. They have seen too much attention to each other and the excessive intervention of their lives takes them into struggling.

Of course, I did not get carried away by their arguments. I just listened to them quietly. When I intervened in the conversation, I watched from a distance and thought carefully that a bigger fight would take place.

The debate began at the beginning of the conversation with Bob. He lived on the street for about two years.

"Hey, Robertson, where are you from? I lived in Quebec and came here two years ago."

"Quebec is so cold in winter, not to mention

that I used to see people who were frozen on the road often when I was there, now I'm getting older and I have come to such warm Vancouver because I hate the cold."Bob began to talk without hesitation about himself, Stories about living with a family in Quebec, and the fact that they lost his wealth because of gambling, divorced his wife and broke up with his children and came to Vancouver alone.

However, Robertson did not respond to Bob's saying.

He did not intend to start the conversation from the beginning.

He tried quietly alone to be solitary, but Bob wanted to lead the conversation regardless of Robertson's thoughts. I thought that their conversation would soon end with a fight.

"Hey Bob, I do not care about the past story, it's a big homework for me to live for the day, and I'll tell you one thing, Bob, you feel so proud and bragging about yourself. Here, there is no anyone to receive your boast."

At Robertson's frank say, Bob's expression was a little exciting.

"What, Robertson, what did you say? You've never gotten a home; you've never made any money. What do you know?"

"Bob, I'm not a gambler like you, I've never been addicted to gambling, I've never been divorced, and I think I've lived a life that's better than you, except that I've been alone on the street from the start. I did not feel like talking to you from the beginning."

Bob tried to get him into the controversy in a very angry tone, whether Robertson could not get rid of the feeling he was ignored by the frenzied atmosphere, but Robertson first got rid of his seat and the two disputes ended with it. Here, these things happen often. There is no way to keep each other open. It seemed that they were the way to survive here.

The autumn here is short and the winter is long. Last winter, there was a lot of snow and cold days. I could not find comfort in people's mind as cold weather. There was no attachment to life. It would be better to say that only one day lives with only one life. Bob and Robertson were people I did not know well.

When I saw their eyes on the street, it was just seeing and sharing light greetings. I also did not care where they lived and what they were doing.

I was in a position to survive here. For a long time, my homelessness has ruined my body, and I had to live my life day by day with loneliness and hunger. I thought a little brawl was also a luxury here. The past was not necessary.

Only the present was a great concern to me.

In those days, it was a remarkable change for me that I was a homeless, drug addict, alcoholic like them, and that now I am living this life transition.

Chapter 2

I HAD BEEN living on the street for three years. In the fall of the year, there were many days when it rained as much as any winter, and it felt cold even during the night. It was hard to endure if it was not wintering coats.

I could sometimes avoid cold with a warm cup of tea provided by volunteers. It was painful to fall asleep on the street even though it was autumn, not winter.

At that time, I could not have spent the night in complete spirit. Sometimes, the drugs and alcohol that attracted and tempted could not easily be rejected.

Not only me but other homeless people living together on the streets were in same situations, too.

They were highly dependent on drugs. I have lived like this for three years, and my body was not normal. The after effects of the drug were painful. All of the stomachs were worn out, bitterness was flowing in the mouth overnight, and kidneys and liver function were ruined, so it was hard to stand a day.

At that time, my age was over forty, but the actual appearance seemed to be old enough to look beyond 50's. Three years ago, I gave up all my life and came to this place. I am not home here in Vancouver. My hometown was a city called Chilliwack where I could get from Vancouver in about an hour and a half by car.

Chilliwack was a beautiful place. Along the high mountains and the Fraser River, the people settled here to find gold mines. There is a place called Hope in 45minutes drive north of Chilliwack. It was the place where people who came down the Bible route to find the gold mine and named the people who came down the land, and the area of Mission just below Chilliwack was also a biblical route and became a conduit for the miners and the Christian gospel they brought. There is also a border going south to the United States. The place was named Sumas.

It was a place famous for the resort because of its natural environment, surrounding high mountains and beautiful rivers. I was born there. It was an aboriginal band. Many Aboriginal people lived in the past. During my childhood, many Aboriginal inhabitants were there. I was not white since I was born. It was indigenous.

Here it is First Nation. There are three words referring to Aboriginal people.

First Nation means a nation that originally settled in North America. The eastern Alberta and Saskatchewan are dominated by the Metis.

They are a mixed race between aboriginal people and France and Indians. I was a First Nation of which blood did not mix. My ancestors crossed the frozen Alaska ice continent 15,000 years ago and settled here in Chilliwack.

My ancestor called Stolo nation. I was also born in Chilliwack through my grandfather's grandfather and spent my childhood there.
My childhood grew up in Chilliwack Aboriginal Reserves, and I had lots of memories. My name is le-woot in a native language. It meant brave wolves and bears. Both father and mother were Aboriginal people who grew up there. My father was a fisherman who lived on the Fraser River every year from October to November to catch a salmon herd.

Because of my father's job, our family was always full of salmon food all year round. I liked smoked salmon the most. I can not forget the deep flavor of the salty and sweetness.

I filled them in my pocket and eat whenever I am hungry. The family was a large family. Aboriginal families were a large family.
Usually, three generations lived in one house.

My father and a grandfather, and a great-grandfather also lived in a house when I was youngest.

I was the sixth of the seven brothers; three sisters, two brothers, and one younger sister. I went to an indigenous school in a protected area. All were Aboriginal children. I learned English and Canadian culture there. Long ago, Canada was a land of Aboriginal people. It was a long time before I was born.

As soon as I was born, I became a citizen of Canada and grew up in the reserved area with an identity of Aboriginal people, watching, listening and learning about Canada history. There was no objection to it.

I learned the culture of this place and learned the language with other aboriginal children.

Although sometimes mixed with traditional indigenous languages used by adults in the house. However, after then it became easy to speak and use in English.

It became more comfortable to use English anytime.

Now my traditional language has become a preserved and unused aboriginal language in old-fashioned minds.

I have never forgotten the words of my grandfather when I was a child.

"le-woo (my nickname)! Do not forget your

roots, do not forget the tradition that comes down from the ancestors, and especially do not forget our words! They will protect you wherever you go."

I remember that I answered "yes" to my grandfather's words, just bowing my head. But after so many years, I seemed unable to keep my promise to my grandfather.

My body has become an adult, but my spirit is still on the level of a child. After witnessing the death of my father when I was a child, I was suddenly shut up and confined to my own world, disconnected from the outside world. I was eight years old.

The weather was cloudy from that morning. The rain seemed to be poured out; the sky was covered with a thick cloud of darkness. It was a time for a group of salmon to climb in the middle of the river. My mother told him not to go out to the river because the weather was not good. But he said it was a good time to catch fish now, and he went to the river with his old canoe with some co-workers. At that time, the father's back view is still not forgotten.

After that day, my father did not come back. When I found my father's body in the river, it was ten days later. My grandmother and mother held on to my father's body and wept. The death of my father came as sadness with great shock to all of my family.

I have been an adult since that day and could not cry well. Maybe it's because I forgot how to cry.

So I did not know how to comfort others and to be comforted. The absence of the father made me so.

It seemed all the time had stopped. I felt like I could not go forward because of the fog forest where I had to grow up and the way to go suddenly. It was difficult to live as First Nation. No matter where I go, I could feel the invisible discrimination against First Nation.

I went to secondary school, but I could not continue my studies.

I mixed with other races and studied. There was still discrimination there. If I did not get better than others, discrimination against First Nation would have visibly choked me under the same conditions.

I did not study very well. I could not follow my department studies. The school board said you should graduate secondary schools in order to be treated properly in this society.

But six years, the period felt too long for me. I thought that I would need a different English name than the name I had in my childhood to live in the future. I thought about my name. I suddenly felt like Jim was a good name. It was easy to call and to memorize. And most of all, Jim was the name of the television cartoon character I loved so young. After that,

"Native Jim!" people called me.

I liked the name very much. So, instead of the name Le-Woo, I was living under the name Jim. After that, I got away from school naturally, and by the time I was in 11th grade, I did not go to school for the winter semester.

And as a small fast-food restaurant employee in the neighborhood, I started to work in the community and started to live economically independent.

Here, 17years old is a person who can be economically independent on his own. And whoever can choose their own life. I decided to go to society early and live my way rather than graduating and going to college.

My mom did not oppose my decision. Since the death of my father, my mother and brothers have suffered a great deal economically and mentally. These reasons have led me to live alone from home.

I decided to quit my school and start my social life before other students of a school. In order to do that, I thought I had to get out of the Aboriginal Reservation Area that I had been living since I was young. So I rented a room in a shabby apartment near Chilliwack downtown on condition of sharing with another roommate. Monthly rent was about $350.

Twenty-five years ago, the wage at that time was about $3-5 per hour. I worked eight hours a day and at night I washed the dishes in the restaurant for about two hours. I could earn about $40 per day. I worked for about 6 days a week. Sometimes it was enough money to spend leisure time watching movies I liked in one of the old cinemas in the downtown once in a while. I worked at Tim Horton, a representative coffee specialty shop in Canada.

I still could not forget the day I first interviewed the HR representative.

I saw a job advertisement in a local daily newspaper and made a simple resume and visited downtown Tim Horton. Many people in the shop were having coffee and talking. I sat down at the table with the staff at the guidance of the clerk. He was a man of about forty. He looked at my resume for a while and talked for the first time.

"Are you First Nation, your name?"

"It's Jim."

"Jim, is this your real name?"

"No. The original name is Le-Woot, and Jim is my English name."

"I understand, but you did not graduate from secondary school, and our recruitment conditions are asking for a secondary graduate."

"I know well, I quit school for family reasons, I do not live in the Aboriginal Reservation now, I rented a room near the store, I am ready to work hard if you give me an opportunity to work I will do my best."

He listened to me for a moment and fell in thought. And He opened the speech.

"Okay, I think it would be nice if you could work here once because you could not graduate from secondary, so you have to start with the minimum hourly wage from the beginning, and you'd better start with cleaning the store."

"One thing I want to ask is that in order to work in this society you have to know that the basic conditions are secondary graduates. I wish you could continue your studies while working."

I was delighted that I had the opportunity to work here rather than say that I would continue my studies. And the interview was over and the start of my social life could start with the Tim Horton shop cleaning.

I still could not forget the experience of cleaning up at Tim Horton and washing the dishes at the restaurant at night for the first time in society. First, my economic situation has improved. At that time, I had no idea that I should save my money in the bank for the future. Once I made money, I had spent all that month.

The remaining money except the rent was used for entertainment expenses.

With friends who left the school of the same age, we gathered and drank and played on the day when there was no work. I also watched my favorite movie all night long.

It seemed that the somewhat oppressed emotions that had grown up in the family since childhood exploded at once. There was no need to be redeemed by anyone. In the world, I felt all the freedom alone. I spent my twenties as that life continued.

Chapter 3

I WORK IN a small shelter where Hastings meets downtown Vancouver. Compared to the past, it was a changed life that can not be imagined at all. When the weather gets cold, we provide sleeping places to the homeless at night and small lunch and daily necessities for them in the season. This morning I came to this place regularly and began to deal with what I needed to do. The first person waiting at the door was Henry, who was 65 years old. He always handed me a smile towards me.

"Good Morning, Jim! How are you?"

"Good morning, Henry! How are you doing? How did you get last night?"

"Jim, it was so bad last night, the weather is second, the streets were loud all the time, you know, Kessie, the girl from Alberta."

"I know Kessie, she did not come to the shelter for almost one week, but for what reason did she go to the police station?"

"As you well know, the police found out that

she was selling illegal drugs, not just drugs, but drugs that were prohibited by law, and they were involved in some theft and were taken to the police station. You know this time will be uneasy to her."

I have warned her before. Do not buy drugs or sell them. She had a bad habit to steal something. Probably she would have stolen at the shop. Her age is now in mid-forties, but she lived on the streets with her friends who met in prison without a family and sometimes lived as a drug addict and theft and prostitution. I advised her to escape from her bad life and legitimately live a normal life in society, but she refused my offer each time. I was very upset when I heard that she was caught by the police last night.

After a moment of thought, I looked at Henry. He can tell me the news of homeless people. He could be seen as a messenger on this street.

"Thank you for the news, Henry, and I'll have a warm cup of coffee in a little while."

"Jim, thank you, Jim, thank you, I have a wish for you when I look at you. You were like me a few years ago. You have been changed in many ways and I am really looking at it. What happened to you? I really want to know about your changing."

I hesitated for a moment how to answer the question of Henry. Before, he had asked me the same question. I told my story every time. Maybe he did not listen to it or heard it, but he could not remember it easily. Now Henry is an alcoholic. He was so addictive that he would not be able to survive without drinking a day.

That morning I smelled liquor from head to toe what he drank last night. Alcoholics can be considered very weak memory.

There are many people who often forget and have not only gastrointestinal disorders but also mental disorders. Henry is one of them. I know Henry is an alcoholic.

So I do not get angry with every word he says. I tried to understand him and tried to help a lot. I wanted to fill the necessities he needed. Henry and I are about 20 years old difference.

If he was married young, there would have been a son like me. Information about him was that he had a family, a wife, and children.

At one point, however, he began to fall into gambling, and even his business was devastated by gambling costs and then divorced and moved to Vancouver alone.

He could not withstand loneliness and has been living on alcohol since then. His hometown was Prince George, which could be reached by car eight hours north of Vancouver. That place was cold and snowy in winter.

Everyone who comes here has a story. There are

many stories that they want to do. They tell their own story. They like to have listened to their own stories more than others. It means that they feel a lot of loneliness.

Henry is the same. He is indifferent to all the processes that I have changed and have worked here as normal people. No matter how much I talk, he does not remember. But Henry always tells me his story. He likes to tell his story so much that I memorize all the processes he has repeated over and over again. It is because it thinks that the sadness and the pain of the past. They are comforted a little to talk about his saga. So I listen to their stories well.

Sometimes I share my story with them and check our presence with each other.

I gave Henry the necessary supplies, sat with him for a while, and had coffee together and talked about what happened last night. And the work on Kessie was recorded in the Shelter note.

We must record the actions of homeless people who have been helped here.

I have to go to the police station where she is in the afternoon if necessary.

People in here often disappear without notice even when they are visible for a while. So I get the information I need from a person like Henry and take photographs of those who visit the shelters in advance and record them with personal information.

There are frequent disappearances here. When the disappearance happens, I have it in advance and attach photos and information to the shelter sign here so that others can see it.

After finishing all the work, it became 11 o'clock. Now is the time to prepare for lunch.

Of course, lunch is ordered on a daily basis and served as a donation from several organizations.

There are so many organizations that there should be no duplication of dates. I took a look at the service journal today where I will be serving lunch.

Today is the day to prepare lunch at a group called the Dove Ministry. The Christian group and leader was Mrs. Lee, a pastor who came to Canada and was a Korean. She was about 65 years old.

She has been doing this ministry for about ten years already.

All of the shelters here are run by the Canadian Lutheran Church. The place was purchased from the denomination, and all the volunteers were made up of Lutheran Church saints.

Of course, I am also one of the saints of Lutheran church. Although I have had faith for about five years, since then I have participated in worship and all service activities. And I got this job by introducing the church. When I think of all of these things, I really appreciate my present life. A little over 11 o'clock. Pastor Lee looked at opening the door with carrier some food. I immediately rushed to her and opened the door.

"Hello, Pastor Lee, how are you?"

"Hello, Jim. How are you doing? It's nice because the weather is so warm today. It was so bad because rainy season."

"I think it looks easy to walk a little today because both of knees wasn't good in the past,"

"It's a bit easier to walk today, perhaps because it's associated with the weather, it's hard in bad weather but it's less painful in the knee than in the cloudy weather."

"I hope you will be able to recover quickly."

"Jim, thank you for always serving in this way." Today's menu is a salad, potatoes, and beef.

"Volunteers are already waiting for you to help me out with meals today."

"Yes, every time I come here to prepare for the people and thank you for your help, I hope to be a good service today."

I went to the restaurant with the food that the pastor had prepared and rushed to prepare lunch with other volunteers. The people who come from various places every day to prepare food and serve can come close to them in the streets a little more.

The more these people are, the less lonely the people of the street will be. Most of them who join this serving are Christians.

Of course, non-believers also come and serve, but they often serve a lot in the church. There is a desire that the homeless people know their minds well. As a person who has lived on the streets for a while, I know their hearts better. I was eager to do my best and to be able to take away all my heavy things of the past.

By 11o'clock in lunchtime, I opened the front door of the shelter. They greeted each other with a greeting and shaking hands with them. I knew their names all. Because I have been a homeless person for a while. Usually, many people visit at lunchtime.

Most of the people living on the streets do not eat breakfast. So we have to prepare our lunch early.

I decided to be 11 instead of 12. Because they were hungry and cold all night, they do not necessarily have to pass the lunch. Some people come alone, but sometimes the parents are poor enough not to buy food for young children, often bringing their children to have lunch. There are many pieces of bread in the shelter that have always been donated. So after lunch, they always took all bread for their supper.

After many people eat at once, they have to deal with the rest. I can not do it alone.

Of course, even the rest of the volunteers do it themselves.

They will do their best in each area, from cleaning the floor to collecting garbage.

I am deeply impressed by such features and appreciate their dedication.

I am always thankful to the volunteers, but there are people who are especially memorable.

His name was John. He was a young man now in his mid-thirties. He did not marry.

But now there is his girlfriend who comes out to serve together. John was a homeless person, a drug addict, a few years ago. He was abandoned by his parents in childhood. His parents divorced when he was 7. In the end, he lived as a 15-year-old independent through his foster mother.

However, while attending secondary school, he was involved in a drug offense and spent seven years in prison as a prisoner. He had released again, but he could not overcome the temptation to commit a crime. He spent half of his life in prison. Even after he was released, he lived on the streets as a drug addict.

But he received the evangelism of the pastor who served for street people. At first, he refused to accept the faith, but the love of Christ ultimately led him to discard the street life and make him completely new. Now he is training for rehabilitation. He also works part-time in Bottle Depot on weekdays.

And he comes to the shelter here and takes care of people with me. It was a moment when a person changed. I thought he could not be changed when I saw him. There were no days to live in a clear spirit almost every day because of a drug addiction. He was even taken to an emergency room with an overdose of medication.

However, he is now totally transformed and seeks to find the most rewarding thing in life and to live again. Whenever I looked at him and found that it could be a Christian to anyone. Everyone who comes here has the potential to be transformed like John in the future.

I was born and raised as an indigenous person. I lived in a confused identity while wandering, feeling discrimination in blame and despair. Everyone lives in this world feeling lonely. I also feel lonely because I am human. It is a reality that can not be denied.

I sincerely hope that those who visit here will be comforted their loneliness.

Now I am not alone. But only a few years ago, I thought I was the one with the most lonely and sad destiny in the world.

Chapter 4

I COULD NOT get up easily the next morning because I was having alcohol with my friends last night. Even though I set my alarm at 7 am and fell asleep, but I could not get up that day. I felt morning sunshine through the windows, and then I opened my eyes and it was already 2 hours after I had to go to work.

"Damn it, it's 9 o'clock, I should have gone to Tim Horton's store by 7 o'clock."

I did not eat breakfast and hurried out of the house with only a robe. And rushed the bicycle and headed to the store. Fortunately, the house and Tim Horton store was about 10 minutes away by bicycle.

After arriving at the store, I opened the door and rushed in. I could feel the manager staring at me with cold eyes as I opened the store door.

"Manager, Sir, I'm sorry, I could not keep the time to go to work."

"Jim, it's a lot later today, it's not the first time I've ever seen it, so if you do this a lot, it's very difficult for us. Jim, I said, you have to keep working time. There are a lot of people who want this job even if you do not."

I could not talk back to the manager's scolding. All his words are right. A perception was not the first time today. I often used to invite my entire friends home for a party on the day they were paid. Yesterday was such a day.

"Hey Native Jim, do you understand me? You have to decide today whether to continue with this job or to quit now and find another job."

I had to beg the manager.

"Manager, I want to take this opportunity only once, and next time if I will do this again, I am willing to quit."

"Jim, you must know that this is the last consideration I can give you, and I'll deduct it from paycheck later today. Get back to work right now."

"Thank you, sir, I will be careful not to happen next time."

I went back to my seat and changed into a clerk uniform. I took the bag and garbage bin and started cleaning the inside of the store. Cleaning in the store was my job.

It was two hours late, so the donut powder

left by the guests on the table inside the store, and there was a lot of garbage.

I am the only one of the shop clerks to be the First Nation. There are 15 clerks who work today.

Among them are seven Filipino immigrants, one Chinese, one Korean, and five white people. Most people seem to have biased prejudices.
Of course, I do not care about the gaze that they see toward me.

People think that Aboriginal people are being treated well by receiving state subsidies and receiving free education and medical services.
They know generally that Indigenous people are often lazy, irresponsible, and just like those who do not do things in the house and do not clean their houses.

But their idea is entirely wrong. There may be such Aborigines, but not all of them. My dear father was very diligent. His attachment to his family was strong and he had a commitment to life. He lived harder than anyone. My father always organized the house well. I watched such a father by his side.

I also seemed to start to look like my father when I started my life. Sometimes I wander in my life and hang out with my friends for a while, but I want to think of it as a youthful experience.

Anyway, I do not like a misunderstanding

about the indigenous people.

I often feel the invisible discrimination towards them. Aboriginal people are distributed all over Canada.

I have often heard from my grandmother that it is not easy to live as an indigenous person on this land.

Every year among the Aborigines, sacrifices are celebrated for the souls of the Aborigines, who are missing or sacrificed by past conquerors.

The fact that there are 3,000 Aboriginal women missing between the years 1980 and 2000 is a fact every Canadian person knows.

There is no way for us to know where they are now or the victims of any crime. However, the strong prejudice against Aboriginal people is still deeply rooted here.

Sometimes these thoughts push me further.

So, it seemed that I was trying to win a tough reality by drinking alcohol together with my friends with a deviant act and smoking cannabis sometimes.

The first step toward the world that started in Chilliwack was seemingly smooth, but it was not easy to stand alone. A year or so I was able to earn living expenses by myself.

However, due to my unfriendly life with friends, I was no longer able to work in the store. After the manager scolding, I became more aware of it a few times. Of course, I had to hang out with my friends all night and lose my time to go to work. Eventually, the manager fired me. It was a year after I started work.

Which was a holiday day? Suddenly the phone rang. I felt like I was late for a few days ago. When I heard the bell, I felt uneasy. I was afraid it might be a call from the manager.

I listened carefully to the receiver. It was also the calm voice of the manager.

"Jim, it's the manager. It's so sorry to notify you of your dismissal over the phone like this. Jim, you do not have to come to the store anymore. I've been patient with you so far. But I think our patience has reached its limit.

For a few days, I will send you paycheck to your address. You've worked hard for a while. There is one thing I want to give you advice. Go back to school. Go and finish your last grade and graduate. It's what you need right now for your future. It is the advice as your life senior.

I could not answer the one-sided dismissal notice. I just had to listen to all his advice silently. It was all right from beginning to end.

I could not resist because it was the result I received for not doing my job well.

I turned off the receiver and suddenly I lost a word and looked at the ceiling. I slowly turned my gaze toward the window.

It was raining outside the window. It was a rain that kept falling for several days. I approached the window and took out a cigarette and blared it with a lighter. The outside scenery was blurred due to the long sigh and the wind at the window. I stubbed out a cigarette and went back to bed to sleep.

I wanted to forget about the dark reality rather than being tired, and I wanted to go into bedding on the bed after the habit. When I was scolded by my mother when I was a child, the habit of going into the room was hiding in the bedding on the bed. Then it was self-reliant behavior that I could escape from the reality that I did not want to encounter for a while. But even if I lie back on the bed that day, the impact on dismissal was big.

I was worried about my future thoughts for about 30 minutes and I went out to wear clothes again and went out.

Outside, the rain was getting thicker. I went back and walked along the street with an umbrella. I went to the cocktail called Blue Day, which I usually go to often.

I opened the store door and went inside. There were people in the bar who came in from the rain and talked to each other while drinking. There are a lot of people looking for a cocktail bar when the weather is so cloudy and rainy. I was one of them. I slowly walked to where the bartender was.

"Hey, come on, Jim, you're alone. What's wrong with your face?"

The man who worked as a bartender was Tom, a young man who was ten years older than me. I often stopped here to talk with Tom. Because I was able to get various information about life through him.

"Tom, have you been doing well for a while? It's a little depressing to me today; I got a notice from the shop I was going to work in. I do not have to work anymore."

"Oh, no, you should ask the manager for one more chance."

"Of course I tried, but this is not the first time, I've often been late, maybe because he can not take it anymore and I have to quit because I can not do anything."

"I can understand your feelings when I hear it. I'll give you a bourbon here."

Tom filled the empty glass with bourbon. I said thank him and slowly began to drink the bourbon.

"Jim, what will you do in the future? Do not you have to get back to work?"

I could not give any answer right now about his words that I should seek work again. He also told me that I had to go back to school. But until then, I was only young at the age of just 19, and it was a time when I did not really understand the meaning of studying for the future of people. If I had been in the mid-20s, the same age as Tom, the idea of graduating from school might have been stronger.

At that time, I was not able to hear others' advice to have to return to school. I did not listen carefully to Tom. I was focused on how to live and worry about the rent next month, and what to eat and live. I have not saved any money in the meantime. I have consumed all of them as I earned. When I think about it now, my life at the time seemed to be very hard and not ready for the future. If I go back to those days, I would never live that way. Anyhow, I drank as much as I could at the cocktail bar that day.

Of course, I called my friends who were not alone and drank with them.

Now it seemed that I spent all my money on drinking with my friends. It was because I had a feeling that the stress of unemployment would be solved a little.

Since I left the store, I did not break up with my friends and bought more alcohol and cigarettes at a nearby convenience store. Then I went home and drank during all night with my friends, and fell asleep on the floor of the living room. All I could count on was friends and alcohol. There were several friends, and my best friend was Bob.

Bob was a friend I met while I was working in the store. It was one year older than me, but we could easily become friends because there were so many similarities with thoughts and preferences. He quit his job before me. He graduated secondary school but did not enter college. He wanted to learn skills first.

He was interested in cars so he wanted to work as a mechanic later on. It seemed that there was a clear dream for the future. The only difference is that he graduated from school and I did not graduate. But he could not learn skills. He wanted to be a mechanic, but it seemed to him that he lacked sincerity. It seemed that he enrolled in the institute to study automobile maintenance and worked hard for a while.

But he did not get much. He often talked about how difficult it was for him to learn so much technology.

I could only tell him what you want to do. I realized that there is a big difference between what people think and what they actually do.

In fact, Bob was my roommate. To save the rent, we used two beds in one room.

Since we met at the store, we agreed to share the room together. Maybe we have had a lot of influence on each other. Living was not as easy as we thought. Bob also lost his parents when he was young.

As we met in a shop that felt so lonely and shared the room with me, we spent more time together almost every day. We drink and talk, we go to play together. He was a little taller than me. And his mother was Chinese and father was White. His appearance was similar to me. He had a slightly Aboriginal look.

The next day I woke up and it was already 11 o'clock. As I looked to the side, Bob was still asleep. I woke him up.

"Bob, get up, it's 11 o'clock already."
He turned around and talked with a low voice.

"Jim, I'm tired, we've stopped working, so let's sleep a little longer."

"Bob, I'll get up first, so you wake up. It's too late today."
I asked Bob to wake up and walked to a dining room and drank a glass of cold water. I had a headache that seemed to be broken because of drinking alcohol last night. Bob turned around for a moment and I heard a snoring sound as if he were sleeping again. Suddenly I felt hunger.

I opened the refrigerator door and it was all food and butter and milk left over.

I poured milk into the cereal and ate it instead of breakfast.

I could forget my hunger for a while. I have

not been to work since today. I will be able to rest for a few days now, but I am worried about food for rent in the future. There was no money left in the pocket. First of all, I thought that I would have to go to the labor office near to get the allowance for unemployment as Bob got up. Here, the rights to workers are relatively well-guaranteed.

In other words, if you lose your job right now, you can get a subsidy for a few months.

At breakfast, I first tried to contact the labor office listed in the phone book. I picked up the receiver and pressed the number and waited for a while.

"Hello, is this the Labor Office?"

"Yes, have a nice day, what can I do for you?"

"In fact, I was unemployed and called to apply for unemployment benefits."

"Please tell me your birth date and name."
I told my name and date of birth. They entered information about me and answered that I can receive unemployment benefits on the spot. I promised to go out that day after thanking you. And I hung up the phone.

I told Bob if he woke him up.

"Hey, Bob, please get up. I have a place to go today."

"Jim, where is that place? I am very tired

now."

"It is the labor agency, and since I am unemployed, I will give unemployment benefits until I get a job there for a while."

As soon as he heard my words, he began to rise from his seat and begin to dress.

"Then they'll give you the unemployment benefit, Jim, I'll follow."

Chapter 5

IT WAS RAINING outside the house. Even if I did not have an umbrella, I did not have any problem because I was wearing the usual hood.

Bob and I took the bus to the place where the labor office is located.

It was in a downtown neighborhood where I could go by bus in 10 minutes.

We waited about 15 minutes after we registered at the information booth, and a representative appeared.

"Hello, is your name Jim?" "Yes, I am Jim, and this is my friend Bob and I have been trying to find out if I can get unemployment benefits because I'm unemployed."

She was blond and white, and she started to look at the papers related to me for a while.

"You are Aboriginal, and you have received subsidies from the government until a while ago, but you were unemployed a few days ago.

"Yes, can I get unemployment benefits?" "Of course you can get it at the current papers, but the period of receiving unemployment benefits may be limited because of the subsidies you received from the government as an indigenous person."

"Are you limited to unemployment benefits? What do you mean?"

"Unemployment benefits are payable, but they are temporary. You can get them in proportion to the salary you have received up to six months, and of course, you have to work in it again."

"Did you say just six months?"

"Yes, it is unavoidable for us, and in order to give you a chance to get started again, you will be paid a nominal amount of living expenses for the time being."

I was disappointed for six months and could not say anything. But I knew that I could live it right now. I signed her documents and walked out of the labor office with Bob.

"Hey, man, I think it's a good period for six months to us. Think that you do not have to work for six months, but you can just sit back and live with your paycheck."

As Bob says, I get exactly $8400 for a total of six months. I was relieved that I did not have to worry about living expenses for the time being. About $1400 a month comes into my account. If it is money, I don't need to worry about rental payment and buying groceries. But this idea did not last very long. It took me a few days to apply for my unemployment benefit and my $1400 was deposited into my account. I was a little relieved after checking the amount. For the time being, I did not have to worry about food expenses. But after a little time, my thinking began to change. At first, I thought I would save my own money and find my work.

But Bob and I began to gather opinions about investing this money and making more profit. It was a foolish idea to think about now. Where did I invest with $1400? At that time, I did not know that it was a wiser idea to find work while living with the money.

My age was not in the 20s, so I did not know the world that much. There was a lot of trouble in the world that should not be done only by a young spirit. Throughout the day, Bob and I began to look at what we could profit from looking at the local daily paper.

If I looked at some of the most typical things, there were a lot of things to consider, such as buying a favorite lottery for Canadians or lending money to people who need a little pay and picking up daily interest. First of all, Bob and I went straight to a convenience store selling lotto. And I bought a Lotto Max of 50 dollars. Perhaps every Friday I bought Lotto Max for tens of dollars. Of course, there were some of them, but I had never seen more than 4 digits of seven digits. It seemed impossible to try to reverse life with lotto. Honestly, The thought that I would enter in the probability in one of ten million times was a completely stupid idea when I came here. I began to spend all money in a month without temperance.

Of course, I recognized the job, but I was difficult to find the job because I could not graduate from secondary school and because of prejudice against Aboriginal people. Such a life had been repeating for an or two month. And in the end, I went where I should not go.

Now I came to think that my life would not have been so difficult if I had not been there at that time. It was Bob, not me, who wanted to go there. It was a casino. It was a place called a gambling place. I had never thought about it. I could not forget Bob's words at the time.

"Hey Jim, you can sit there and make a lot of money." "Have you ever heard of that place?"

"Where's Bob?"

"Just go and enjoy the game. Have you heard the name of the casino?"

"Casino!"

I listened to it for a moment and fell in thought. I had no idea what Bob was talking about.

"Bob, the casino is the place to gamble, probably more to lose than to get the money."

"No, Jim. If you think so, nobody will go there. Maybe I'm going there because there are people who pick up the money."

"But I'm not old enough to get there, how old can I get in?"

"From only 19 years old. Jim, when is your date of birth?"

"My birthday has already passed. January was my birthday."

"Well then, you are 19 years old, and you can get in. Let's go, Jim."

I could not refuse him. Maybe I did want to. I would have given my nervous excuse.

"All right, Bob, Let's go there." Bob and I went to the hotel-casino near Chilliwack by bus.

There was a bit of rain scattering and the weather was not bad enough to feel cool.

As we approached the entrance to the casino, two sturdy men, who seemed to be asking for identification in front of the door, came to see us and talked to us.

"What are you doing here?"

"I've been trying to enjoy some games here."

"Could you show me your ID for a little while," he said.

I showed them a driver's license I got a year ago. After confirming my age and address he gave permission to enter. Of course, Bob, older than me, passed through a simple check.

"Thank you."

"I hope you both have a good time."

As soon as I entered the casino game, I couldn't stop talking. The gaming arena had a trendy pop music craze and was crowded with many people. A person holding a whiskey in one hand and a person playing a poker game, a variety of games were unfolding in front of you.

I approached the slot machine game that I listened to. Before I came here, I was interested in slot games. I was a little excited because I was trying to play it for the first time.

At first, I had about $100. Today I talked to Bob first by investing in a $100 game. The basic slot game finally started.

"Hey Jim, you do not have to be nervous. Slowly bet what you want in your mind and as much as you want."

Basic slots often start with a small amount of game time, so people can not leave easily in front of the game machine. And there are some other versions of dividends. Based on this, they begin to demand maximum coin play for the upper jackpot. I could not easily leave the game. At first, there is no law to lose anyone.

I also did not lose in the first game.

I played a game with 100 bucks and won $500. Bob invested $200, leaving 700bucks profits. It seemed that I never had so much money in my life. It seemed like a dream.

"Bob, this is the best thing I've done," I said, "I left five times as much profit as $100."

"Jim, I told you to come here, we can not afford to lose. If we lose games, we just think that we have a life experience each other."

"Yeah, you're right; I think I'm really good at coming here."

"Now, let's go out with this money and drink with it."

"Yeah, I feel so good today. Let's go out and have a drink and enjoy it."

I walked out of the casino game room with Bob. Then we went straight to the bar. We ate and drank to the dawn the next day, and celebrated the victory of the day.

In fact, it was the first time that I made so much money at once. I was in such a world that I doubted my eyes and ears. I did not earn a big sum like everyone else, but I earned five times. Now I think I was too naive at that time. The feeling of getting paid once did not disappear after that day. It was hard to go back to everyday life. Whether at home or on the streets, the excitement experienced at the casino game room remained unforgettable.

I should have never returned to the casino gaming ground ever since. But already my mind and thoughts have been lost to casino slot games. Bob was also like me. From that time on, the two of us have had more casual access to the casino. Of course, the money that goes into the game was covered by unemployment benefits.

The amount of money invested in the game began to increase. At first, it was $100, but over time it increased to $300 and $500. I even had more than $1000 in a month. Bob was the same. I could not think of paying rent. The number of months that can receive unemployment benefits gradually began to decrease and the rent began to be pushed.

Of course, if we get a lot of money for the first time in the game, the story will change. Unfortunately, more and more days have passed since I won the game. It was already late when I regretted it. I and Bob had reached the level of gambling addiction.

Chapter 6

ONCE WE stepped into the casino, we could not easily get out of there.

The idea that we have now come to realize that the first time we won the money was that the sweet temptation of gambling was the bait that was thrown at us. Just because we won money, the thrill of gambling continues to produce addictive chemicals called dopamine in our brains.

On a day when I did not go to the game room, my mind was empty and my mouth felt dry. Once we entered the game room, it was unexpectedly fun, lost our money, or made some profit, and we almost fell in love with gambling. I remember someone saying that.

Once gambling or sex has fallen into addiction, our brains continue to produce dopamine. The most misunderstood of people is that they feel happy when dopamine comes out. But now that

I think about it, it was a lie. Dopamine is associated with addiction. It is dopamine that stimulates the brain when gambling. Something similar to dopamine is serotonin.

Serotonin is not associated with addiction. Serotonin is a kind of reward that comes from happiness and small things in the ordinary life.

I am grateful for small things, and serotonin comes out when I am happy even though I get a small income.

It is not as stimulating as dopamine.

I was foolishly thinking that what I felt when I was gambling for a while was a feeling of happiness. In the end, in the world that made a mistake in the moment, Bob and I could not get out of the way, and we got into the path of addiction. The six-month period for receiving unemployment benefits has passed.

In the meantime, I've wasted all the time playing gambling, and I could not get jobs. I did not pay rent for three months. I received a notice from the landlord asking me to leave the house. The only remaining money in my pocket was $200. Bob's situation was the same like me. Nevertheless, we could not stop gambling.

It was a bubble-like hope that this opportunity would get a lot of money. If I win the game once, I would have thought that it would be a waste of time and money. Eventually, all the money was lost, and Bob and I had to be forced out of the house.

There was nothing that came with anything. The owner of the house had put all the money in the auction. Bob and I went out of the house only to say that I was sorry to the landlord with only clothes and belongings. It seemed to be the middle of March when the winter was just over and the spring was just beginning.

But Chilliwack's March still had a lot of rainy weather, and the temperature was very low. We had nowhere to go.

"Jim, where are we going now? Do you have any place to know, friends or family?"

Bob also had no family to depend on. But I had a family that remained in the Aboriginal Reserve. There were brothers and relatives, but Bob was different from me. He had no place to go.

"Bob, do not do this, let's go to my brothers, we can not sleep in the streets like this."

"Jim, where are the brothers living now? May I go?"

"I have to go and ask for it, but we can not stay for a long time because my brothers are not in good economic condition, we can only stay for a few days."

"Thank you, Jim, I'm sorry to tell you I told you to go to the casino at first, I'm sorry."

"Bob, it's okay, what will happen to us anyway?"

"Thank you so much for saying that."

After I relieved Bob, I decided to go to my sister's house in the Aboriginal Reserve. It was near the Fraser River, about two hours by bus from Chilliwack. My sister still lives there with her family.

Not enough money, but she also helped others in the fishing season to catch salmon and make money from canned factories to support her families.

Because I haven't been in contact with her for a long time, but she's the first person I've ever been to since I was a kid and she was kind to me.

My sister's name was Powoo. Meaning is a girl to dance well. Literally, the sister performed the traditional dance of the Aboriginal people very well. I heard a lot about adults saying that I will live according to the name they gave me from my childhood.

Sister Powoo still enjoys the traditional dances on the day when the Aboriginal festival is held and enjoys the villagers and tourists.

I was a little nervous when the village where my sister lives nears me. I was not going to go alone, but with my friend Bob. Obviously, the two of us may be burdened by the situation of my sister's poor economic condition.

But now we have reached a dead end. I went to my sister's house to find a place to stay for a few days now. I informed Bob of some facts he should know.

"Hey buddy, maybe we can not stay in her house for a long time because her economics is not that good, there are five nephews and they are still in school."

"Does she have a husband?"

"No, he died a long time ago."

"How did he die?"

"It was an unfortunate traffic accident, he walked in the night with a drink, he was hit by a truck and died on the spot, my sister got married at 20 and she was alone at 30."

"I do not think it's going to last long, I'll be back for a while or I'll be out."

"Bob, do not tell my sister that we have gambled. My sister hates gambling, drug and liquor."

"Okay, I will not tell her."

We slowly began to enter the house where the sister was. It was raining. The yard was soggy with clay. The figure of a house has not painted it yet, so the roof and walls are very old, and the board is shaking in the rain wind and it seems to fall soon. It was because there was no adult man in the house, and it did not cut grass yet, and it became a lush grass field as it was.

We looked at the inner reaction while pushing the doorbell outside. The door opened for a while. It was Powoo sister. It seemed that her face had become worse without seeing it for three years.

"Are you Le-woo? My younger brother? Is it my brother Lewoo who left home three years ago? It's been a long time. Come on in."

My sister warmly welcomed me and Bob. And she brought us in.

The nephews were already in the living room watching the television, and it smelled delicious soups and meat cooking on the stove of the restaurant. I felt a little hunger.

"Come on boys, come to uncle Lewoo."

All of my nephews were full-grown. They also warmly welcomed us.

"Uncle, how have you been? It's been a long time."

It was nephew Harry. He was in the 10th grade of secondary school, and he was a child who played with me often as a child.

"You guys are hungry? Let's have dinner together." "I appreciate, I will introduce my friend, Bob, he was a roommate, and I did work together."

"Come on, Bob, welcome." "Thank you for welcoming me, I am a very good friend of Jim, I heard a lot of things through Jim. You are a good dancer of traditional."

"Well, is Jim saying about me like that? I like to dance very much. Anyway, here we are, we have dinner together and we talk."

We ate at a dining room, eating beef, soup, and mashed potatoes.

It was a wonderful evening. Sister Powoo kept telling me all the while we having foods and asking a lot of things she wanted to ask me.

"Jim, what have you been doing for three years? Of course, I knew your best regards on the phone, but I wondered a lot about what you were doing."

"My sister, I've been doing well for a while. I quit school and worked at Tim Horton, where I met Bob and I stayed close to each other like brothers."

"I'm so glad you're doing well, Bob, thank you very much, and we didn't have enough time, so we couldn't afford to look back on how my brother was living."

"Jim and I have been doing very well over the years, so do not worry about it, because Jim is so nice that we can easily hangs out with other people and makes friends."

"Sister, can Bob and I stay at this house for a while? I came out of the house I was living in. I would like to stay at home for a few days while

I'm looking for work for a while."

"Jim, we are always welcome both of you, but I think we should use the room with your nephews because the rooms are small"

"Thank you, sister, enough for a few days. We will find jobs ASAP.

Sister, Powoo always treated me kindly. Compared to other siblings, it was the most comfortable sister who had no burdens.

Maybe I could feel the warm mother's emotion from my sister. It seemed that I could stay close to my sister. Anyway, I was glad to have a place to live for a while.

I used the room with two young nephews, and Bob also used the room with another nephew.

Fortunately, my nephews were all male, so there was no pressure to use the room. Traditionally, many Aboriginal families live together in the house. So it was natural for brothers to have the same sex in a narrow house.

It was an unfamiliar culture to Bob, but I naturally used my nephews and rooms without such a big rejection.

We had a great time sharing that story with my sister and nephews that night in the living room until late. It was a time to feel the warm atmosphere among the family members who felt like it.

Chapter 7

IT SEEMS to be meaningful to live here on Hastings Street. I am deeply satisfied with my life now. My age is now over 40, but I am very happy now compared to the dark moments of the past. Life in chaos and disorder is always insecure. My past was like that.

Unplanned life gradually destroys everything of my life. I spent a decade in prison as a criminal, and after leaving home, I could not abandon my sinful habits, begging on the streets, taking drugs and giving up all my life like other homeless people. But now I will not try to live such a life. When I met the miracle of my life at Hastings, I still can not forget it.

The moment that was clearly imprinted in my memory changed all my life. The people here live a day without any purpose. And suddenly they pull out of the world by adapting to a clock that tells the closing time of their life. Their lives are like migratory birds.

Without any promise that it will disappear for a while and then meet again on the spot. But Hastings Street has its own philosophy. Those who have come to the end of life, their lives are our warning and the way to another world. I found a way here from the end of life to a new world. I am very happy compared to other people on the street and called a lucky man by street people.

The reason I like it is that I learn every day why I should live in the world. There is probably no rewarding thing to be able to help others. The streets are full of people who need help. They are all weak characters. The fact that my life has changed so much that I can help them as I see people fallen on the street gave me great comfort and responsibility.

I wanted to be a Good Samaritan from the Bible. In the New Testament, a person falls on the road. He was the one who met the robber on the road. It was enough to be taken away and to die. No one tried to help him fall. The scribes and religious leaders just passed by. Who were they? Those who lived the hypocritical life that Jesus most disliked. But the Samaritan, a Gentile, was different.

He pitied him and cured the wound. In addition, he asked to take care of him. I wanted to live as such a Good Samaritan. As Hastings's

Good Samaritan who helped those who fell on Hastings Street. Even 20years ago, I did not know the purpose and meaning of life. I was born as an indigenous people and spent my childhood under unseen discrimination. People think that indigenous people are originally lazy and uninsured.

They know aboriginal people who receive a subsidy and benefit free of charge without any purpose are seen in people's eyes.

I also grew up in such prejudice. I may have been made to such prejudices too. But now I look completely different from what I feel. I work as an employee at the Hastings Self-Help Center. And living in this building and having meals with people from other streets in the cafeteria is getting paid for fair labor. If anyone wants to live a new life, this country provides an opportunity. When I was young, I would get up late at 11 in the morning.

I lived in a fuss and drank with my friends all night. However, now at exactly 6 o'clock in the morning, I wake up and open the center door and prepare breakfast with volunteers.

And at 8 o'clock, I give to the people who visit here the necessary supplies along with last night's greetings, washing clothes and guiding them through the necessary space to take a shower. Then rest for a while and prepare lunch with other volunteers. It is free time in the afternoon.

At that time, I go out and participate in an adult education program to gain a secondary diploma and study the subjects required for graduation. After studying, return to the center and prepare for supper. During the cold winter season, the shelter is opened here to create a space for sleeping and management.

It is run by the Lutheran Church and is supported by the government. Of course, I get a wage from them.

It is money that earns the minimum wage per hour but can live alone and save a little. I am grateful for all my life. Some time ago, I met a man who could not think of anyone at the center here. It was Bob, who broke up a long time ago.

At first, I did not recognize his face. I thought it was not him at first because it was a face that changed so much.

It was a very cold winter night. I have prepared a good room for sleep here and opened the door of the center, a middle-aged man in a cloaked dress almost getting drunk and staggering.

"Who is this? My friend Bob is right. It must be the friend who broke up a long time ago. Do you remember me?"

"Who are you? I can not remember."

"Look at me carefully, you have not forgotten my face, it was a long time ago that we lived in Chilliwack together in a house and became a friend."

Bob tried to take a closer look at my face. It smelled strongly of alcohol and his body could not stand because of his wounded legs.

"Oh, now I have a little thought, you are Jim; you are younger than I am, Jim, my friend Jim, good to see you."

"Bob, your face has changed a lot."

"Jim, I've been here for Hastings for about a week now, and I've been in prison for years."

"Prison? When and why did you go there?"

"Well, it's a long story; I can not tell you what I am now.

I drink a lot of alcohol, and nowadays it's hard to have a day without alcohol. Jim, you look so good?"

"Bob, I was a homeless person a couple of years ago, but not now, so I'm working here normally to help people, I'm glad to see you. Did you eat any foods?"

"I have not had supper yet. It's so cold that I think I'll have to sleep here today."

I grabbed Bob's hand and sat on the table for the first time.

And I brought the food left in the dining

room hastily warming by the microwave.

"Bob, I have a lot of hot soup and beef, and some bread. You have to eat it first, and I'll prepare for showering to wash your body and sleeping well."

"Thanks, friend"

Bob emptied dishes and bowls like a person that he couldn't eat anything for a few days.

I brought him to the showroom and the laundry room in the building. I handed donated coat and underwear to him, cleaned his body and prepared to wash off the dirty clothes. After the whole process was over, I sat down at the table with Bob for a while and talked together before sleeping.

Bob slowly took a sip of warm coffee. His eyes were staring at the ceiling with a slightly blurred vision as if he had not been drinking yet. I said to Bob again.

"Bob, how have you been? Why can not you walk so well? What happened?"

"Jim, I was in prison all the time. A few years ago, I was caught stealing cars again. I hurt my legs a little bit trying to avoid the police chasing me."

"Oh, did you have leg injuries seriously at that time?"

"Yes, both legs were broken, I had my legs knee pinched and operated, but then I cannot walk well because of the aftereffects of the injury I got five more years in the trial. I remember it was about 20years ago that you and I were in prison for the first time, and after another release, we committed another crime, and then we didn't meet each other after you first got out."

"Bob, you're right, we've been in prison for a while, but now I'm not that time."

"Jim, I've seen a lot of you, You've changed a lot, it's not Jim before, it's a lot better to see, but I'm not. My body has been ruined. It's not healthy, there's nowhere to live, and I have to get out of here and should live on the street tomorrow unchangeably."

"No, Bob, you can live a whole different life like me, enough to get out of the bad way of life, I've found a new way of life, and now my life is so happy and satisfying."

"I envy you, how can you tell me if I can be like you?"

"Of course, do not let me tell today, I will talk to you only a little rest, tomorrow I want to speak with a clear spirit."

"Thank you, Jim, for giving me such a favor, it was like a miracle to meet you, remember? After we first went to the casino and lost money, we could not get out of gambling addiction.

I was kicked out and stayed in your sister's

house for a while."

"Of course, you remember, and you and I were both feeble-hearted. Now that we are older, we should be able to live a new life. It's not us when we're young."

"You're right, thank you."

I made a bed for Bob and returned to my quarters on the second floor of the building and was prepared to sleep. And before I fell asleep, I read the Bible, knelt on the Lord, and prayed.

First, I prayed that he would bring me into the Lord's arms. After the prayer, I opened the diary and thought about what was happening on that day and went on to write my diary. All of a sudden, past things came to mind. The things I felt after meeting Bob today and the things I once lived with him began to come to mind in my long memory.

Now, when I look at the relationship between Bob and me, I have many thoughts. It was Bob who became my friend when I was young. I was born as an indigenous person and grew up here, and Bob was a close friend of mine. I was not lonely because of it. But I also have this thought.

If I had not met him, we would not have gone the wrong way together. In fact, since I met him, my life has been getting worse and worse. I thought I should not, but I went into a deeper quagmire that could not escape. The idea that I should not have gone to the casino gambling along with him, the regretful things of the last day when I could not get out of the gambling addiction and set up gambling money until I committed a crime together.

I did not know then that the first button was misaligned and that next buttons would then be misaligned. The existence of Bob is a person who is entangled in a relationship of love-hate for me. Various thoughts about it made my head more complicated. One thing is clear, however, that I still think I should guide him who cannot come out of the dark corner of society.

I prayed for him for a while. And after a while thinking about what to do tomorrow, I went to bed. I asked Bob the next morning whether he slept comfortably last night first. Of course, he said that he could sleep warmly. I had breakfast at the center with Bob. And with our newly changed clothes, we went out of town.

It was Friday morning for the weekend, so the people's footsteps seemed busy. I went to the Pentecostal church where I worshiped every week. There is no worship on Friday.

But the reason for going there was the store next to the church. The store was a shop selling recyclables. It was called Second-hand shop or Thrift shop here. The reason I went there with Bob was to introduce Bob to the manager there.

He told me last night that he was looking for a job. But no one had given him a suitable job because of his criminal records.

The church was located in the city center. Church built in a red brick building. It was a church with a tradition about 40years old. The ivy was wrapped around a red wall and reached the spire of the church. Apparently, it was a very nice building. The Thrift shop was located on the opposite side of the church.

It built a small prefabricated building where it got lots of donations to run. Every week a lot of things were donated, so we needed a worker to sort it out and display it in the store. Bob and I opened the store door and went inside. A lot of things were arranged in a very large space.

"Welcome, Jim, how is you? It's not Sunday, but what are you doing here?"

Stevens, who works as a manager at the store, welcomed us. He was a retired soldier in his mid-60s. He was serving as an elder in the church and was the general manager of the store.

"Hello, Elder Stevens, I came to introduce a person because it needed someone to work in the store."

"Even if it is not, I need someone to work with. Thank you, is this him?"

"Yes, his name is Bob, he is a close friend of

mine, Bob, and this is Elder Stevens."

"Hello, I am Bob, and it is a pleasure to meet you."

"It's nice to meet you, too, said Stevens, I've been looking for someone in this store. Have you ever worked at shop?"

"Yes, a long time ago I tried to sort things out in the store." "I believe that Jim is the person who introduces me, and I will give a job to you," he said.

"Thank you very much."

Bob continued to express his gratitude to him. I was grateful to Elder Stevens. Because he believed that much me and hired Bob. I briefly spoke with Elder Stevens separately. Of course, it was about Bob. He needed rehabilitation now, and the church had to pray for him and help him get back into the Lord's arms.

Elder Stevens agreed with me. We agreed that it needs a person to meet the environment and warmly to change. After the story, we went out with Bob. And then back to the center where I work. I decided to use the room with him until he started work and resumed the room again. The Canadian government is helping people in their homeless lives to rehabilitating in many ways.

Anyone who is willing to quit his homeless life and gives himself the independence of his own will give him the room and living expenses he needs. I decided to find someone who runs a recovery house near the center for Bob.

Recovery house is literally 'house of recovery'. It is a common living space where many people living together.

Of course, the government subsidizes the necessary room and board. The problem is a commitment to rehabilitation.

I asked Bob again. I asked if you could settle your life and start a new life. He made it clear to me that I had a will to start a new life.

I was pleased with his pledge. I thought I would have to find someone to run the house of recovery for him.

It was all the grace of the Lord that we both came together again. If it were not his grace, I and Bob would probably still be wandering the streets and committing crimes. The past days have come to mind again. Twenty years ago, when I left home with Bob after a few days at my sister's house, things suddenly ran past my head.

Chapter 8

THE COLD rain that prompted the winter was flowing down through the window.

When I started to like the rainy night. The sound of falling down against the wall of the prefabricated buildings makes me feel calm.

Then quietly guides me to the world of meditation and compassion.

I'm looking at Bob's face with a deep sleep on a floor with a mattress that only one person can lie down on. Tomorrow, I will meet with a friend of the restoration house who will come to the center for lunch occasionally. It is to ask whether Bob can live together in the house.

I opened my diary that night and recorded what happened in the day.

And for a while, I began to write down my memories and reflection on things of the past.

(Past recollection)

I remembered that we had stayed at my sister's house for about ten days. It was a very long story. It was 20years ago from now. She went to work every day and worked in a canning factory until late at night. My nephews played their part by sharing all the housework while my sister was not at home. My sister told me to stay at ease but I could not. We came to her house because we needed space for a while but I did not want to continue to live. Bob also did it.

We were mostly at home during the day. My sister and the children were out of the house because we could only live in a very quiet and comfortable place to both Bob and me. And at night when my nephews and sisters came in, we both quietly walked out of the house and rode the bus and walked around the downtown.

I was always full of thoughts in my head. I felt sorry for the money I lost and the next opportunity I thought I could possibly hit the jackpot. It has been about the day when we should leave. I told Bob that we should leave my sister's house now.

He also did not object. I could not stay at home any longer. It was because I was sorry to my sister that I did not do anything (and did not recognize the job, of course). I told my sister that I should leave a house now. Of course, my sister said you could stay longer, but she could not keep me from talking. Perhaps the sister would also have felt uncomfortable with her in the heart. I finally asked my sister. I was asking if I could borrow some of the money now.

When I left, I thought I should have some money to live on. But surprisingly my sister lent money to me. It was about $2,000. It seemed like it was a little money saved every month. My sister seemed to have lent me the money to live right away because she thought I would leave the house. I said to thank her. And ten days later, Bob and I said goodbye to my sister and came out of her house.

As I say goodbye to my sister, I still can not forget the sister's eyes looking toward me at that time. It was as if she was anxious and full of compassion, just like a child on the water. I may have been heavy and confused because I had relied on my sister since I was young. I ate breakfast with Bob quietly and got out of the Aboriginal Protected Village.

It was because there was not as good time as morning to get out of the eyes of the village people. Because the indigenous people usually sleep until late in the morning. I had to leave the village before others could get up. We took the bus to the city. There was a $2000 in the pocket borrowed from my sister.

This amount was enough money to buy a room and food for a while. And I was looking for work during that period. However, the idea did not happen at that time. We were still in great need of losing our money. Of course, our steps were towards the casino.

"Hey, Jim, I do not think we should go to the casino right now, but it's like your sister's hard-earned money, and she'll be very disappointed if she finds out that we go to such a casino."

Bob was right. But I was already in a casino game. I was so addicted to gambling that I could not get out. Bob was also similar to me. I just knew that he was saying that because of his sorry feelings to me and my sister.

"Bob, let's go to the gaming room once, not to invest $2,000 in the game, It's not all about investing 2,000 dollars in games. And if we play a little game we can get our money, once we get a lot of money at once, we can pay back the debts we owe to my sister. Let's just go this time."

Now I have become convinced to persuade Bob. My foolish idea was that I would return my foolish thoughts to my older sister, earning profits of several times.

What a foolish idea to think about now? But at that time I had fallen into a gambling game that I could not get out of.

We took the bus again to go to the casino game room. There was a lot of thought on the bus. I was a bit of expectation. Maybe this time I got the feeling that I could get a lot of money. Bob and I opened the casino game room and went inside.

At the door, people watching the guard greeted us as if they knew our face and opened the door.

"Come on, Jim. Have you been good all along? I have not seen you for ten days, so I wondered what happened."

"Tom, have you been so good? I stayed at my sister's house for about 10 days. How is the atmosphere inside the game room today?"

"It's always the same, I think it would be nice to say that the feelings of those who are lucky and those who do not are so intricately intertwined and riding on roller coasters of life."

"Thank you, Tom! I feel like the game is going to be good someday."

I went into the game room with Bob. I sat in front of my favorite slot game as usual. Bob also sat in front of other game machines and started playing. From the beginning, I invested 100 dollars. And slowly pulled the bar. The picture started to come back with loud music, and after a while, the picture card I wanted was set. It was a pleasant departure from the beginning. The money I got from putting $100 was about $250. This was a very good start. I was cheering up I could not stand the excited emotions.

"Bingo! Hey, Bob, look at this."
Bob showed his thumbs and sent a message of congratulations. I started to fall back into the game with his gaze behind. I already sat in front of the game console and felt a little nervous and relieved.

This feeling was a common phenomenon for addicts. It was a kind of self-help that actually appeared to those who were addicted to the game. Perhaps I will withdraw from this game machine again.

However, it is such crowded minds that the mind is troubled and the gambling game machine grows in front of the eyes and wants to go to the game room.

Now all these moods are gone. The feeling of increasing amount of money began to disappear. The $100 bills looked small enough to look funny. It is a terrible addiction symptom that gambling brings.

I have no idea while I'm in the game. I felt that I existed only in the world. There is no discrimination against birth and no worries about the future. This game machine in front of me now seemed to speak for all of me and even to my future.

However, once the game is over, there is a sense of frustration in my heart. Why did I come here again? It was regrettable thoughts: I do not want to come here again. I do not know how much time was spent in the casino game room. It is impossible to tell whether it is daytime or late. When I was hungry, I solved the meal simply at the restaurant inside.

Eventually, in less than two days, I lost all my $2,000 money. After losing money, I came to Bob in the game room, and once again deep regret and despair came to my heart. It is because the days of the future were dark.

'How should I live now? There's shameful at sister's home. I can't go back,'

Bob also had a similar idea. I asked Bob if he had any place to go. But there was nobody in the world that was left alone in the world. We were forced to sleep over the cloak that night in a corner where we could avoid rain and wind in a park.

It was really rainy that night.
The temperature was also very cold. I thought of a warm soup. But I did not have anything already. There was only a few loonie in the coin pocket for one dollar. It was money to buy only one bread. We bought a bread at a convenience store ate it on the park bench. When the next day dawned, Bob and I visited the center for

nearby the homeless people.

A shelter where people can sleep overnight was not open yet, but the morning breakfast could be provided for them. It was a breakfast of hot soup, bread and bacon that day. It was a satisfying meal for us. We ate breakfast together and decided to think about how we would live together by drinking a cup of coffee from there for a while.

"Jim, I'm glad I was able to eat this morning here, but I can not resist the temptation to go back to the game room after playing the game."

"Bob, I'm like you, too. The idea of the game keeps coming out of my mind, and I have a lot of worries about what to do next. "

"Jim, we do not have a place to sleep right now, so I think it's better to stay here until the shelter here opens."

"I have the same idea as you. If I had not been here, I would not have been able to eat a day."

I decided to stay in the shelter with Bob. I could not find a better place to avoid the cold here. But the mind was always uneasy. Because there was no place to work right now.

There was no place to work for penniless people like us. Above all, it was a big reason to be seen as people who could not believe us. It seemed to be such wandering birds without a nest, loitering around the streets all day long.

What we can do is pick up the bottle and change it at Bottle Depot. Bottle Depot was mostly done by the homeless people. But it also takes a lot of time to walk around the city.

Bob and I started walking around the street all day. Then we began to rummage through the garbage cans in front of the store even the house.

Sometimes we had to hear people talking to their children: boys, don't live like those homeless people over there without any purpose of life. Then, when we found an empty beer bottle or a drink can, we screamed as if we had won the game. We received 50 cents for an empty beer bottle. This was $1 for two bottles.

We walked around with dozens of kilometers a day. We started collecting bottles one by one in a black garbage bag.

On some days there were about 20dollars a day, and on street festivals, more bottles and cans could be collected. We did not save the money that was collected. We just used it to drink or buy food.

We always wanted to play casino games, but because we did not have as much money to play games, we were always thinking with our heart.

On the day we received the living allowance that comes out about once a month from the government, we went to the game room without hesitation. I received nearly $200 a month. But the money was soon lost in the game, not even a day. Such a life repeated every day.

The day was uneasy. I did not think that my life was wrong at the time.

Just thinking that this is my normal routine, I spent only meaningless days.

Chapter 9

MOVING AROUND the streets with Bob and searching the trash can pick up bottles for a while. When I think about it now, it seemed that I had done it for about six months. We came to the shelter and slept. Winter was able to avoid the cold because it was sent away from Shelter and ate meals with simple food.

"Hey, Jim, how long should we go to collect this bottle?"

"Well, maybe this winter will go and a warm spring will come, now we have no place to go and Shelter is our only resting place."

"Well, it's very hard to walk around the streets every day, but there's a lot of sick days with blisters on my feet someday, Damn it! I missed the day when I went to the casino game. I do not have as much good time as gambling to spend time and stress out. Hey, Jim, when do we get a subsidy? Let's go to the casino instead of trying to collect bottles."

"Okay, Bob, I thought so too. Every day, when I collect my bottle and sell it for at least $10, it is all over if I buy alcohol and food."

We knew that the first Monday of each month was the day we received the subsidy. For a homeless man on a street without a residence, $200 was a very big money. Of course, if you do not stay on the streets and are in a recovery house where several people can stay together, you could get about $600 for the room rent and food. However, entering the house of recovery is subject to many restrictions.

Because they eat food jointly, they are not free to clean. And while you are almost inhabited, you should also avoid taking any alcohol or drugs. In other words, it is subject to many restrictions.

Bob and I hated it, so we deliberately lived on the streets.

Of course, now I am very regretting why I have not entered the house of recovery. If I had found a way to get in there and become self-reliant, I think I would not go to that place with Bob. Such a place was a prison. I was a prisoner at an early age. Of course, there was a reason to go to prison. I want to talk about it now.

Bob and I rushed to the casino gaming room immediately after receiving the subsidy. And I started playing games. But I lost more days than picking money. Such good luck to other people did not come to us either. The two of us were very disappointed.

We cursed the world where can't give us a chance to get lots of money. We had to break all gambling and start new. But we could not do that. Eventually Bob and I were planning to do something we should not do.

We spent the winter in the shelter. And it seemed that it was March. It was not that cold anymore. I could sleep well at night.

And it was not so cold during the day, so I had to walk around to pick up bottles. Spring is not a fast-coming country, but the weather seemed warmer that year. It seemed that it was time for us to slowly find a place to live on our own. Just like migratory birds have to move south for winter. The shelter was just a place to stay.

Bob suggested that we go out with him first and I did not refuse him. We had no reason to stay in the shelter anymore. But I still do not go out every day, but when I got subsidized and played games and all the money run out, then I got out of the street and collected bottles.

That day was about the same. Still, the chain of gambling could not be broken. People did not look good on us.

They did not welcome ourselves who did not work, but we did not care about their eyes. It was a way of life, not just thinking about it. Because living in the consciousness of the other's eyes is to live with stress in oneself.

When I was hungry, I ate and slept everywhere when I came to sleep. It was a series of life with gambling, eating alcohol and no planning. In the meantime, I always dreamed of a good fortune.

I slept on a park bench at night I dreamed of gambling and dreaming of a luxurious life envied by others who paid lots of money.

It was a dream to live a good life in a good house with pretty girls every day. But once we came back from a dream, the reality we met was not at all. People have accused us of being weak persons, irresponsible homeless people for their lives. We did not care at all whether they looked at us like that. I guess what I thought was how horrible it was now.

The vague idea that everything will be different over time was our life motto. It was a fanciful imagination that all this would come with a once great opportunity in gambling. But it would take a lot of money to do that. Because I had to pay a lot of money to get an opportunity to win the game. With a subsidy of $200, it was only a paltry sum.

It was a little money that would disappear in a

day. We knew that we had to have a lot of money to invest to get a big chance.

One day when the weather was warm and the spring was brisk, I talked to Bob first.

"Bob, we can not carry bottles or cans for so long, so we have to hold on to something, what do you think?"

"What are you talking about, Jim?"

"I mean, we can not live for a long time by collecting government subsidies or bottles."

"You're right, Jim, sometimes I think about the loss I've lost at the casino, but I do not think we have any other alternatives."

"Bob, think about it." The reason we lost it in the game was that we had a small amount of money.

"I think you're right, but we do not have a lot of money.""So I mean, Bob, let's just close our consciousness and have a great day."

"What is the matter, do you mean to take money from somebody or do something illegal?"

"Yeah, Bob, that's what I'm saying, let's just do this one time, but of course, it's a crime, but it's a big part of it, it's back to the lost person, and the rest is starting out with us."

Bob looked surprised for a moment. But he did not panic about me. He asked again in a more calm state than I am.

"Well, Jim, what are we going to do with it?

Should we go into the rich man's house and steal expensive stuff, or shake a store or bank or steal a luxury car and sell it?"

Bob seemed to already know my thoughts. Just as he waited for me to speak first.

"Hey, Bob, I've been watching closely."

"Where is it?"

"It's just a few blocks away from here, it's not that busy, and it's where people do not come by even though it's evening time."

"Where is that place? Jim, tell me, this is a nervous one."

"It's a small bank. I think it's probably a branch, and it does not have a lot of staff. I think it's cash in the evening when I see it. I had seen employees put money in the safe last time; it seemed to be hundreds of thousands of dollars."

"Well, what about the bank?" "Yeah, it's a bank. No one has as much cash as a bank, so it's dangerous, but it's best for us. What do you think? Bob?" "Jim, this is a very dangerous idea, something I have never expected before, and I have no guarantee of success."

"Of course, it's difficult, but there's a feeling that we can succeed," he said.

"So, what do you have to go to the bank? Just a bat or which weapons?"

"I do not think I have a pistol right now. It's

hard to get it. How about an imitation pistol from a toy store?"

"Imitation pistol?"

"Yeah, a fake pistol! It's the same as the real thing; it's easy to get confused. People are probably terrified and they will be deceived."

It was frankly frightening to me to say this. So far I have not even thought about crime. I instantly remembered the face of my parents and sister from my head. I feel sorry for my family who are genuinely concerned for me. But at that time I was not a whole spirit.

I was full of unusual thoughts in my head. I would have been crazy about the daily life for six months, getting a bottle that was repeated every day, going to the bottle depot and getting a little money.

Anyway, then I could not make normal thinking and judgment.

I was just full of thinking about money in casino games right now.

I thought it was a momentary moment for people to change their lives. It's like a summer night's dream. I dreamed of constant my social status ascension, every night a nice car, a house, and a wonderful life that no longer borrows money for the family.

So I thought I should not, and I tried to convince Bob to do whatever it takes. Bob has been living in such a world without causing big problems.

He did not have the guts to commit a crime except to enjoy a little alcohol and gambling. I did it too. I was a boy who was so weak that I could not kill the living salmon that my father had taken from my childhood. Now that I had planned such a great job, it seemed like the nightmare at that time. I had to persuade Bob to do whatever he wanted. I could not do it alone.

"Okay, so you've got a fake pistol, how can you find a way out of it, and one person has to wait outside to get away quickly?"

"Bob, I do not think one person needs to wait outside, just go in and go out together, because once we can not get a car, let's steal any motorcycles on the street. It will be easy to get away from people."

"A motorcycle? I drive a motorcycle a little better. Okay, let's try it."

Together we traveled around the city to find a motorcycle to steal. We walked a little, and a pizzeria shop came into sight. Nowadays, pizza is being delivered at home.

Every store has a delivery motorcycle or a small passenger car.

The pizza house we saw was a shop that was mainly delivered by motorcycle.

We were far away and gazing carefully at the store. It seemed to be about three or four hours when the store clerk was finished delivering and was entering the pizza house.

He moved very busily. We saw him enter the store with the motorcycle key left intact. That was the moment.

We quickly stole the motorcycle. Of course, Bob was driving. The motorcycle started to move away from the store with a roar.

The shop clerk had slipped out of the shop, but we had already disappeared. We shouted together and quickly drove the motorcycle out of the city. We ran away for a while driving the road. The cool wind hit the face and made me feel refreshing. In my memory, this was the first time I stole a big thing.

I've ever stolen small cigarettes and drinks in a store for a while, but what I stole this time was the biggest thing in my life. Of course, there was a bank robbery except this.

"Hey Jim, how are you feeling?"

Bob, who is driving the motorcycle in front, asked.

"Bob, I feel good, what about the clerk's face now?"

"Maybe he must be scolded by his master, haha" Bob smiled and spoke. I thought the embarrassing and sad expression of the clerk at the moment.

I thought he might get fired from the boss.

At that time we did not realize that while we were glad it was another person's misfortune.

Chapter 10

THAT NIGHT, we did not go to the shelter. I got to the pub where I often go with the money I have. There we drank alcohols all night and discussed what to do next.

"Now we have a motorcycle, and tomorrow we have a lot of work to do. Let's go to the bank first and see what happens to it after the situation and things are done."

"Jim, what should we do if we have stolen money after we've done it? Should we divide it in half?"

"Of course, Bob, we should divide our stolen money in half, and let's enjoy the life of each of us, whether it's investing in games or buying anything we want."

The pub door closed at 2am. We could not stay in there anymore. We came out. There was a bit of rain on the outside, but it was not that cold. We drove a motorcycle to a place where we frequented the nearby park. It was a place to avoid the rain. We laid a small blanket on the floor and started drinking again. And suddenly I lost my mind. I began to fall asleep deeply.

My body was not that cold for a long time. Suddenly my body became warm. And the situation that cannot distinguish whether it was a dream or reality was unfolded in the eyes. It was a place I had visited when I was a child. It was a protected area inhabited by my native Chilliwack Aboriginal people. My hometown was seen. I saw a canoe that my grandfather enjoyed. The canoe was painted with indigenous patterns. The pattern was salmon. Sometimes Aborigines painted salmon in canoes. It is drawn with the desire of ancestors who want to catch a lot of salmon.

It was such a beautiful picture. I started walking toward the house along the coast where the canoe was placed. My house was seen from afar. It was a beautiful house made of oak wood. In the yard, the salmon was hung in the sun. My grandmother was standing there and smiling at me. And the puppy Kuhn, who I liked, ran for me. It was a small, hairy black puppy. He looked at me and was glad and rushed and hugged me in my arms. I stroked Kuhn.

I looked at Kuhn and looked toward the house. There was a sister who played with me when I was a child. She always looked at me with warm eyes. She was a good friend of mine and a mentor in life. My mother was cooking delicious food in the house. She was baking the bread that the locals used to enjoy. My mother always baked me some bread with honey. I have enjoyed the bread since I was young. She looked at me and said,

"Le woot, my family loves you very much, and we always pray for your well-being life no matter where you live. We hope you to meet a good friend and to select the right way."

I could not answer my mother's affectionate words. I was just bowing my head down there.

I was able to wake up from the dream. I turned my head for a moment and looked at the side. Bob was still awake from sleep. The day began to brighten gradually between the park trees. I began to shake Bob.

"Bob, wake up. The day is coming."

"Let me sleep for a bit, I am very tired, we will have to wait a few hours to be in the morning."

At Bob's saying, I could not urge him anymore. I lay down and thought about my dream.

'Why did my sister and mother appear in my dreams? Is it because I was planning illegal things?'

I began to get complicated by various thoughts.

But I did not change my decision of yesterday. I also took a motorcycle and made plans in advance. Now it is time to go into action. This afternoon Bob and I will head to the bank we were aiming for.

Dreams are nothing but dreams. This is my first and last chance. I can not live like this anymore. I had a desire to live like others. After tonight, I do not have to go to the garbage cans for bottles again. I do not have to sleep on the street in the cold. Maybe tomorrow morning everything will be changed. My determination was firmly established. I woke up earlier than Bob first, and when I thought about what I had to do today from the beginning.

After we got up we divided the pieces of bread we had put in the bag and ate it for breakfast. I visited the shelter for a while. It provides free coffee in the morning. There was nothing better than a cup of coffee that could warm up the body all night long.

So we used to stop by the shelter in the morning and to drink a cup of coffee and to start the day. Bob and I were drinking coffee and discussed the specific schedule.

"Hey, Bob, let's go to a nearby toy store, and it's time to open the door at 10, and then there's a fake handgun that's almost like a real thing. Let's steal or buy it. Do you have any money with you?"

"What am I going to do;I spent all to put gas on a motorcycle yesterday. What about you?" "I am also penniless. This is so frustrating. Anyway, let's go there. There must be something."

The two of us went to the downtown shopping mall. It opens every day at 10 o'clock. But if we enter that time, it is easy to be detected soon. It should be entered in a time that is mainly used by people. It was because we had to steal at the moment of a clerk's busy time.

So we decided to take some time off. After lunch, we went to the store. The store was very crowded with children and parents who came to buy things. I went to the place where the fake pistol that I usually looked at was displayed. And I took it out and started to rip out the wrapping paper using the moment that people did not see. Of course, Bob wrapped around me with his body and began to turn people around.

I could easily hide a fake handgun in my arms. We quickly ran from there to the parking lot where the motorcycle was standing. I was able to steal a fake handgun successfully. We drove on a motorcycle and headed straight to the downtown border where the bank located. I set up a motorcycle nearby a bank where I can see it well. And put my hands in pocket, I was fiddling with a fake handgun. I had a heavy and cold feeling that it made with iron. It seemed like a real thing. As if I had a real pistol, I seemed to be overconfident.

"Hey Jim, it's so nervous, it's our first time, it's a totally different situation than stealing kinds of stuff at a store."

"Bob, I do, too, but I'm here so I can not just go back." Look at that bank window. How many people are in there?"

"Well, I do not think it has much of a guest right now."

"Well, do you see a bank security officer?"

"Yeah, he is sitting in the chair beside door, a person; I think he's wearing something around his waist. Maybe it will be a real pistol."

"I do not think so. I came to see here once before, but it's not a gun. I think it's a gas gun or an electric shocker."

"I do not think bank security is so thorough, it looks very poor."

I decided to watch the bank side more. It was afternoon time so people did not visit that much. Soon work should be done before the late afternoon when many people visit. I was very nervous too. I was really sweaty in my hand, and I kept trying to relieve the strain by swallowing my saliva continuously.

"Hey, Bob, we have to go inside now. Do you have a face mask?"

"Yes, here you are."

"Now!"

We started running towards the bank together. There was a fake handgun in my hand. And Bob had a pocket knife and iron pipe. We stepped into the bank gate. And as soon as I entered, I cried out in a loud voice.

"Do not move, do not move from now on, and get down on the ground!"

"Get down quickly, you bastards!"

I ran to the bank security guard and hit him with my feet. He was uncomfortable, and he sat down on the ground without power. I quickly took his weapon from his waist.

"Keep quiet from now on and listen to me. If there are people who move a little, I will shoot you with this gun, so do not move on the spot."

There were only about five people in the bank, including security personnel. One of them seemed to be a guest. She was an older woman. It was not a problem. I quickly climbed onto the bank desk and threw the bag at the lady banker, saying to put the money in it. The woman opened it as if she was frightened and began to put money. Bob also threw a bag at another banker and told him to put the money.

It seemed to be about 10 minutes passed. It would not be easy to escape if I stayed there any longer. The two bags were filled with money. I immediately picked up the bag and told Bob.

"Bob, we have to go now. We can not be late anymore!"

"Okay, everyone is down on the ground! Do not move until we get out!"

Bob and I hurried out of the bank. But it seemed to be heard from the police sirens from afar. As we entered the bank, the banker had already pressed the emergency bell under the desk. The situation began to become urgent. If it did not get out of there quickly, the police chase might start soon.

We ran quickly towards the motorcycle side. Bob took the steering wheel. And I sat in a back seat. The motorcycle started to speed up with a roar. As one block passed, I looked back. But a police car has already begun to catch up with us. It seemed that someone had taught in front of the bank the direction we had taken. The situation was flowing badly. We started driving in a narrow alley to get rid of the police car.

"Get out of the way!" "Damn!"

The motorcycle was running on a pedestrian road. People on the streets started to run away from side to side, scared when they saw the motorcycle. Kinds of Stuff on the shelves of the shop shelves and fruit shops on the streets were smashed. All the streets were thrown into utter confusion. The streets all over have turned into shambles.

"Hey, Bob speed!"

"I know, I'm doing my best, but the speed of the motorcycle is not good because it is an old style."

"Oh, damn it!"

I looked back. The police car was still chasing us. By the way, the police car that was one was catching up to increase two cars now. I was embarrassed at the moment. We could not escape to the outskirts of the city because the speed of the police car was faster. We entered the narrow alley again. When we reached some dead end, we decided to flee split for a while.

"Bob, we'll get caught, let's break up from here, let's run away with our own bags, leave the motorcycle here."

"It's a good idea, I think it's better to be scattered."

"Ok, Good idea!"

I broke up with Bob. Then I started to run away carrying my bag. Using the alley, I started to run in the way I knew. It still seemed to sound a siren of a police car from afar. They seemed to have found a motorcycle.

Perhaps I thought they might have started chasing after us.

+ + +

I continued to look ahead and ran away. I heard

sirens from afar, but I did not care. People gave recognition to the village because I was good at running from my youth. I became an adult, and when I was able to do it, I jogged every day. The exercise at that time seemed to be a great help to me. I was breathing for a while. I leaned against the wall in a corner where there was no one and breathed for a moment.

Everywhere was quiet. I did not know about his news because I split with Bob. A few days later, we promised at the only place when I met him. Now I have to be avoided as a safe place. I waited there for the day. I already had a bag of money in my hand. I do not know how much is in it. But until then we knew our plan was successful.

Darkness began to cover the street gradually. Now the police sirens could not be heard. I slowly stood up and started walking. The polo shirt was soaked with sweat on my back. It seemed like I had been walking for a while.

Nearby A & W hamburger shop was seen. It was open 24 hours, so until late it had a light in the store and a few people were sitting.

Suddenly I started hungrily. I slowly opened the door of the store, went inside and ordered a hamburger and a drink and sat down. I ate all the food. After eating finished, then I went into the bathroom for a while and locked the door.

And I slowly opened the bag inside.

It was packed with bundles of $100 and $50 bills. There was no cell count at that moment. It just seemed like $20,000 was in my eye. It was the moment when I touched the biggest money in my life. All of a sudden, there was a worry over the future rather than pleasure.

I did not know where the problem originated. There must have been CCTV in the bank. Perhaps our actions were all recorded.

I was worried that I was chased by a police car as soon as I got out of the bank. They certainly would have checked the motorcycle license plate. It was a problem that they could find us by tracking the number. 'Where is Bob?' I started to get tangled in my mind with tens of thousands of thoughts. 'Was Bob running away safely? Or have he already been told about me to cops after arrested? Do I have to run away to other states?'

I did not sleep on the street that night. Instead, I headed for a motel located a bit away from the city. I went to a place that was very old and the facilities were not so good. Because such a place can easily not the pursuit.

People do not have to search well and do not need identification. It is enough to sign with a fake name. A signboard was seen from afar. I saw the name sunny motel. I was given the room key and gave $50 to stay there for a day. I went to the room number. I went inside and smelled a damp smell. It seemed that it had not cleaned for several days. I simply started to open the bag and to count the money after taking a shower. I guessed right. It contained exactly $24,450. I did not know how much it was in Bob's bag.

But I thought the two bags were the same kind and size, so he would probably have similar money. I did not think I had taken so much money out of my mind. I had a desire to have more than $100,000 in my heart, but I was comforted that I had succeeded in making the first attempt. There was a little scar on the leg. Perhaps it seemed like a wound when I crossed the fence in the middle of the run.

The blood was flowing down. I simply wiped it with the toilet paper around it and removed the clumps of blood. Then, a handkerchief in the pocket was used for hemostasis.

And I didn't know when I started to smoke, but I took out a cigarette and lighted it with a lighter and breathe deeply. I felt like I was getting relaxed. The water in the cup has already fallen and I can not put it up again.

I was suddenly tired. I put the money back in my bag and lay on the bed. How long has it been? An hour hand of the clock attached to the wall was pointing to 3 o'clock in the dawn.

I heard a very struggle between a young man and a woman in a room across a wall. But I did not care. They also thought that there would be a story. I fell into a deep sleep again.

Chapter 11

THE TIME TO wake up from a deep sleep was
11:30 am that morning. It was already half a
day past. I could not feel the hunger so strange.
I promised to leave until noon to a manager of
the motel. It was time to leave soon.

I got up quickly and took a shower and then
went out carrying a bag. The weather was sunny.
It had rained almost every day during the past
week. But today was different.

People were out shopping and enjoying the
sunny weather for a long time. 'Where should I
go now?' I began to roam the streets without my
destination, mumbling alone. A police car was
seen several blocks away.

The moment my mind began to feel nervous.
If they knew my face, I did not deliberately look
into the side of the police car and walked away
from the side alley. I was curious about Bob.
'Could he have escaped from the police safely?'

I thought to myself. If he succeeds in escaping the police, he will contact me soon. Because we promised a place to meet soon before we break up. But I did not hear from him. I became increasingly nervous and uneasy.

We both had cellar phones. I bought the phone almost the same day to contact each other whenever we needed. I decided to go to the park where we usually go. It was to see if there was a trace of Bob whether he went yesterday or not. I took the bus which headed for there. There were not many passengers on the bus.

I almost occupied the back seat alone. Music came out on the bus. It was the old pop music of the 60s, 70s, and 80s that I usually enjoyed. The Beatles' song 'YESTERDAY' began to flow. It was my favorite song. I began to sing along. "Yesterday, all my troubles seemed so far away/ Oh, I believe in yesterday/Suddenly, I'm not half the man I used to be/There's a shadow hanging over me/Oh, yesterday came suddenly ..."

I decided not to regret the past. I decided to concentrate on the fact that this moment will be my memory someday. I have no place to hide. I thought I had lived my life that way. I got off the bus. I went to the place once. But there was no trace of him. It was then. My phone ring started ringing. The phone was a call from Bob.

"Hello, who are you?"

"Hey, it's me, Bob. You forgot my voice?" "No, I was embarrassed because you suddenly called me. How about you?"

"I am doing well right now ..."

"Listening to the voice, I think you are little nervous. What happened?"

"No, I ran away from the police well, and now I'm stuck where I know."

"Where do you know? Where is it? I know if you know where, where is it?"

"I can not explain it now, Jim; can you come here for a while?"

"Hey, Bob, where is it, yeah, I think I can find out, tell me something."

"Jim, I'm doing well right now. Do not worry, we'll meet up and talk about the day ahead." "It's a good idea, Bob, it's a phone call. I think that our choice to move another province."

"Another province? Where have you thought?"

"Yes, I think Alberta is good, and one of my old friends is living in Edmonton, Alberta."

"Alberta? I think it's a good place. Let's meet and talk together. Can you come to this place?"

"Sure, tell me where you are, I'll go there now."

"Thank you. If you get on the highway to the

west from downtown, you'll see a secondary school, and I'll see you at the playground at 2 pm tomorrow."

"Well, good, I know where you are."

"Okay, I'll see you there tomorrow."

I thought for a moment after receiving Bob's call. It was an unusual voice. The appearance of a nervous voicing came up.

I was wondering what might have happened to him. But soon the thought went off in my head. Because he called me. It was only because he proved that he is now safe. I was thinking to leave Alberta with Bob. Because there was no reason to be here anymore. I was eager to start new in the place.

After I made my appointment with Bob, I went back to the city. And I decided to go down to a secluded place and walk for a while. I decided to use a baseball cap to avoid people's attention. Stopping at a convenience store, I went out to buy a pack of cigarettes and a cup of coffee with a $50 bill I had put out in my bag. As I walked the streets, I suddenly heard people sitting and talking together.

"Hey, have you heard about the bank robbery that happened around here a couple of days ago?"

"Of course, it's probably the first time in town." "I do not really know why the world is changing so horribly, it happened in the afternoon, not at night."

"Really, the bank robber might be an expert; it was happened by not the one person but the two."

"Have not the police caught the robbers yet?"

"A news anchor said they did not catch them yet. It needs to get caught quickly."

I suddenly seemed to have two legs twitching. In the city, things that we have done have been a hot topic. Everywhere I go people talk about the bank robbery. Of course, they did not recognize my face. At that time, we went in with a mask and nobody knew anyone. I rather walked up to them and talked with them.

I was not a criminal expert they think. In fact, the habit of stealing small things was big this time. Like a proverb in the old days, a childhood habit goes to an adult. The Bible passages came to my mind. It is a phrase that 'greed conceived and gave birth to sin.' Bob and I were a bit greedy and tried to touch big money. People seemed to think so against us.

I did not get on the bus again. Instead, I decided to walk there.
Because I knew the direction to go there, I decided to go across a large park avoiding people's gaze if possible.

I had a bit of pain in my injured foot, but I had no problem walking. I was soon to meet Bob and go straight to Alberta.

I urged my step toward the place. I walked and looked at the trees in the park. Though not yet autumn, some of the leaves of the tree were yellow, so they could not easily be attached to the branches and fell down without strength.

A school playground was seen from afar. A well-laid soccer field covered with the grass and a playground were seen. I walked slowly to the place. After a while, Bob came out of the back of the school building. His face could not be seen from afar. But something seemed to signal me. But it was too far away and I could not tell if he was saying. I just thought it would be nice to see me. I ran toward him.

"Hey, Bob, how are you?"

Bob showed me what he said, shaking his hand. His appearance gradually began to appear close. We met each other, shaking hands and hugging.

"Bob, it's good to be safe."

"Huh....,"

Bob's behavior seemed strange.

"What happened? Bob,"

"No, but Jim!"

"Why? What's going on?"

Suddenly three strong men appeared and

surrounded me. I guessed who they were. But it is already too late to escape.

"Jim, I'm sorry, I could not help it."

The people who arrested me were the police.

"Jim, I arrest you for burglary, you can remain silent, you can choose a lawyer; let's go to the police station together."

They cuffed my arms. And Bob also handcuffed both arms and put both of us in the car. I could not say anything.

Bob was first arrested by the police after we broke away while we were away. Probably the police would have persuaded Bob.

We would have made a promise that we would meet each other and that if he let them know where I am, and Bob called me, and cops arrested the two of us at a place where we were supposed to meet. In the car, Bob repeated only that he was sorry to me. With the saying that I could not help myself. I could not blame Bob. I also chose to meet Bob. I could not resist. The two of us became trapped in the police station.

It took three days to plan, to do, and end the crime. After all, in three days we have become criminals. It happened so quickly.

I saw a flock of geese flying together in a blue sky through a window of a police car. Maybe they are flying back to where they left. When the leader of a flock of geese which is flying from the front is exhausted, the bird that will become the next leader will come forward again and lead the flock.

When I look at their world, they look really wise. What about our people? Do not I just follow my foolish dreams in front of my eyes? One night dream that no one can achieve. I had a hometown to return. But now I can not go anywhere, I was afraid that everything may be a shameful past. A toddler trying to learn how to walk on the street seemed to take care of one step by holding mom's hand.

Even though she is holding her hand, she is carefully watching the ground.

It may be because she is not used to walking yet. I still feel that I have not learned to walk properly in this society. I only knew that when I came out of this world, I was living on my own. It was not. I never tried to live on my own. Like normal children of the same age, I did not live in ordinary life after graduating from school.
I began to look like a child who was immature. I could not say anything. I could not answer Bob's words that he was sorry when he looked at me. 'What on earth am I sorry for?' He had to do that in that situation. He was caught by the police before I was persuaded. And he called me, and I just went there to meet him.

It has become a past that has already passed,

and now it is only a day ahead. 'What should I do next?' I started to make dozens of thoughts in my head.

'What trial should I receive and what should I say in front of the lawyer and judge? Will I spend years in prison? And how should I live if I come to society and become a past convict?' The scenery of people outside the window looked so happy. But now my appearance is so miserable and sad compared to them. Is Bob thinking similar to me? I looked at Bob.

He also looked out of the window on the other side and seemed to have some thoughts. A police car convoyed us through the main gate of the downtown police station and headed toward the detention center.

Chapter 12

BOB AND I stayed at the detention center for about a month.

There we were judged individually. Although the bank robberies failed, the crimes we committed were serious criminals.

Here, the bank robber is severely punished. Of course, I never used the money I had taken, and all the police recovered it and gave it back to the bank.

Nevertheless, I received a seven-year sentence. Bob also received a six-year sentence. I had to spend 6 and 11months in jail. I soon became imprisoned in Chilliwack Prison.

There were about 400 prisoners in there.

I was assigned to a room used by two other prisoners. One was a drug dealer.

He was the one who had been sentenced to three years in prison for manufacturing and selling illicit drugs. For the first time in my life, I spent

116

most of my life in prison. I spent most of my time in the room, except for one hour of exercise a day.

Bob was imprisoned where there are other facilities. Of course, I have never met him while in prison. Separated from each other and imprisoned.

During the first few months, I seemed to spend most of my time with only lament and grudge against my life.

I was so embarrassed and frustrated that I had to feel self-conscious about myself, 'Why should I be here?'

And myself to live as an inferior in society. I was almost mentally abusive of myself who could not live as ordinary as anyone else.

I had a painful day that seemed to destroy my soul. Because of this repetitive, self-conscious day, my weight has lost by almost 10 kilograms. I could hardly eat the food from the prison. Until then, I thought society was too harsh for me.

I did not understand why it was such a heavy punishment for me because it was not a big money to pay for it and it did not harm anyone. At that time, everything was my central world. I looked at my standards and thought that if I could not understand, it was all contradictory and unworthy.

The day was always repeated there. It started at 6 o'clock in the morning and at the same time arranging the room. I ate breakfast at 7:30 and had lunch at 12:00 and supper at 5:30 pm. The food seemed to be better than ate outside.

It was much better than when I had slept in a cold place, eating simple pieces of bread with the money I had left to sell empty bottles while living a homeless life on the street. In fact, I was surprised at my own life, which is getting easier and more comfortable to get used to in prison. People thought that the creator made it so that they could adapt to the environment and live well.

I sometimes thought how I could live on the street. I did not have to worry about the three: eating, wearing and sleeping at least here. Not only that.

It regularly visits from the outside of the week and gives the opportunity to adapt to society with a good edification program. Sometimes we can talk about troubles through counseling.

I spent most of my time reading books here. Books borrowed from the library were enough to forget the boring time of the place. But there was regret in my heart. Through conversations with people, I could not fill the empty space of the mind. The idea that I should be stigmatized as a criminal pushed me into more pain.

I also thought that I would end my life here. But I could not put it into practice. About a year after I came here, a prisoner died in his room. He was the one who killed many people. It was also the one who chose only weak women. At night, I heard his appeal to the pastor who was doing ministries for the prisoners saying that the victims appeared in his dreams and harassed him. In the end, he broke himself with the sound of conscience and the sorriness of victims.

No one seemed to think that prison was a comfortable place. Everyone was trapped in here and was frustrated and regretted most of their actions. I was like them too. Those who did not have such regrets and sorry feelings for the victims were really like psychopaths.

Such people met here a lot. As if they were proud of their crimes, they had gathered their fellow prisoners at meal times and during exercise times and laid down their own saga. I did not even go there with them.

I thought it was a totally different class from those who enjoy crime. Perhaps those thoughts were my excuse not to accept the reality. They were those who had a desire to sin again after they were released, and I was not willing to hang out with them in prison because of the vague commitment that I would never be a criminal again.

However, the temptation to order and other sins in them, who are seldom in prison, was hard to bear. Numerous crimes are simulated in prison. I could not help but wonder if I could keep them there while I was there. What they sat down to talk about was just a conversation about how they could commit a complete crime without getting caught by the police almost every day.

Drug traders who stayed together in the same room were like them. It is also important to note that when the two of us are in the room together, he always had his own past criminal career, at first; it was hard to listen to him so uncomfortably.

However, I began to pay close attention to his words from whence. Of course, it was not so bad to spend time talking to someone because of the life in prison. I was unaware of their way of life. I spent most of my twenties in prison.

In society, it was the time of young and had a future. At the age when I had to work hard, to love, to have a happy family with my children, but I spent the precious time in prison.

At the most important time, I spent my youth in my twenties while listening to the experiences of other older criminals in prison. I did not know then. I wonder how those times were important to me. Because I did not know, I could not be free from the temptation of crime.

Now, if there is a young man planning a crime like that of my age at that time, I would have told him about my failed experience and advised him not to go the way I had.

"How important is our life to you? Do not spend your spirit and passion in vain when you are young."

At that time, the life in the prison was meaningless. If someone does not lead me to the right path, I wouldn't be able to stop the temptation of crime.

It was about three years after I had been in prison. Maybe it was around Christmas time in December. It would have been Christmas Eve evening in December.

In the pastor's church, several saints have opened a ceremony of Christmas night to the inmates by playing and praise. I was impressed by their carefully prepared programs.

In fact, I have not been to church since childhood. Because my grandparents strictly forbade me going to church.

Aboriginal history in Canada is a history of pain. Because white people took Christianity and used religion as a means to control and oppress Aboriginal people.

Many Aboriginal children were imprisoned and held in concentration camps for Western education to convert to so-called Christianity.

When they lost their indigenous culture and reached the age of 15, when they had already graduated, they had already been assimilated into the heterogeneous Western culture.

When they returned home, it was difficult to adapt to the traditional culture of the Aboriginal people.

Increasingly, the culture of the indigenous peoples became isolated and wiped out. Not only that.

An atrocity that can be put on the children against them was in the school for aboriginal students. Many children were sacrificed. And then it disappeared. It is natural that indigenous peoples reject if they are Western Christian.

I also could not easily go to church because of such influence. Rather, I rejected the church. However, in prison, I have visited such a church that I have never been to. And it was a worship service. It was something I could hardly think of. It has become a precious memory that has been kept in my mind for a long time like a film. Christianity was not an unfamiliar religion, and I knew that it was such a religion that anyone could approach easily.

I still do not forget the preaching of the Lutheran church pastor. The pastor's name was John Rod. He was a gray-haired old man and was about to retire soon. He was the one who dedicated his last days of life for missions to prison inmate like ours.

Pastor John L. Rod showed a sense of generosity that we could see around ourselves before retirement. His back looked a bit curved and he was wearing brown shoes in a tidy suit. He was holding an old Bible. It was a biblical book that made me guess that he would have been together for the rest of his life.

His voice was weak, but his pronunciation was clear enough for everyone to understand. He stood on the pulpit and spread out his Bible and read the Word. I still remember the Bible passages of that time. It was Philippians 2:5-7.

"Your attitude should be the same as that of Christ Jesus: Who, being in very nature God, did not consider equality with God something to be grasped, but made himself nothing, taking the very nature of a servant, being made in human likeness."

"Everyone, this year we are still coming to a beautiful time of Christmas, the day when Jesus came to this earth as a human being, as you know, the God who is God. But when Jesus came to the world, in the image of man, it is the appearance of humility, and people don't like to lose their lives in life. People do not want to see any harm in their lives. People use all means and methods for their own interests. But look at

Jesus. Even though He is God, He has seen the loss for us. Just to save us.

To save you. Brethren, we must live like that. Do not try to have more than others. It is the things that we can not all take when we die. God's kingdom does not need the things of the world. We have to live a life that is willing to suffer for others. It is a blessed life that lives for others rather than me. Just like Jesus."
I could not understand the preacher's sermon at first, but after returning to the room, there was a deep-rooted feeling. It gave me a look at my current image. Through the life of a man named Jesus 2,000 years ago, I was able to see myself now. I did not want to get low in front of others. I could not bear to be ignored or mocked. I did not want to go down.

I did not die but it remained. I have lived such a life that I can stay and harm others. Many people avoided Bob and me.

No one gave us tolerance to us who lived in the streets, who were alcoholic and gambling addicts. So we resented the world and lived a complaining life. And I always blamed my environment rather than myself.
I thought it was because I became homeless and others did not give me a chance. The problem is right inside me, and I always wanted to find the answer from the outside. Through pastor's

preaching, I realized it. Jesus is God. But he was not with God but came down as a man. God humbled himself.

I have never tried to lower myself. Because of my self which never dies, I have made problems in society because of my self - centered thinking. The preacher of the Christmas pastor has given me time to look back at myself. Then I listened to the pastor's sermon every week. I started to attend church in prison for the first time. I also attended the Bible study group.

Through the Word, I realized many things. The time when I stayed there and it was a strong support now. But my religious life was as long as I stayed in prison. After that, I was released from my sentences. But there was no place to go. There was no place to welcome and receive me. At that time, my age was about 31 years old. People like me were already old enough to get married and make a home, but I did not have everything ready.

Chapter 13

THE THICK IRON gate of the prison was opened in seven years. It was the outside wind that met for the first time. I slowly put the things I took in seven years back into my bag and walked along the direction that the janitor was leading.

"Jim, you've been in a lot of trouble here. Where do you go from here?"

In the meantime, Paul who had been close to I in the prison talked to me. He was ten years older than me.

"I have not decided where I want to go yet, Paul, thank you, and I will not forget you wherever I go."

"Take care, Jim, I do not want you to see me again in the future, but if you get out, do you know where Bob is with you?"

"Bob left the place a year earlier than me; I do not know his place yet, thank you anyway."

I bowed to him lightly and came out. Now it was about the end of autumn and going into winter, and the cold rain began down. I did not tell anyone the date on which I would be coming. I am so sorry to see my family.

Especially, I could not inform my sister who was expecting me. I will not visit her in the future. I sat on the bus to downtown looking out the window. In the back seat of the bus, male students who seem to be teenagers were talking. Perhaps seven years ago those students would have been in elementary school.

They will probably have a home to go back to. Parents or brothers who will be happy to meet them. In my heart I envied them. The bus was gradually getting away from the prison. Where should I get off? I thought for a moment. I wanted to see the city after a long time. I saw a signpost about Chilliwack downtown after 40 minutes. I then decided to walk down from the station to downtown.

The rain was getting thicker and I started to walk with my hat. I walked about 20 minutes.

From a distance, I saw Tim Horton, who worked part-time in my late teens. It was good to see the sign. It was still working on the spot.
It was so good that I first worked in society. When I opened the door and went inside, the atmosphere in the shop seemed to change a lot.

The interior and the staff who worked there were not those of the past. Of course, the owner is the same, but the manager of the store was another. I ordered a favorite black coffee. And I drank coffee slowly while watching the scenery outside the window.

The streets were still filled with homeless people and passersby. Christmas is coming soon. It was about a month before the New Year. I thought where to go. I thought the church that I participated in Bible study and worship in prison, and I thought to visit the pastor, Rod. But I could not do it because I wanted to be a burden to him. I did not want to be taken care of by anyone.

The pastor was already old age. Maybe he will not be in that church. I thought he would be moving to a nursing home or elsewhere and be preparing for the end of his life there. I took a cup of coffee and went out again. And I started walking in the city. The landscape of the street has changed a lot. Some shops had the same appearance as they were seven years ago, and buildings with different shapes were built.

I went to the park that I enjoyed. There was a lot of change. But those people seven years ago were not seen. Suddenly I thought of Bob's phone number. I went to a nearby pay phone. Where I knew there was still a public phone.

The past booth color was gray, but now there was a nice phone booth decorated with red windows. I put a coin and pressed Bob's phone number button. The signal sounded after a while.

"Who are you?"

The voice in the receiver was the voice of a woman, not Bob. I thought it would not be Bob's phone at the moment. It was not Bob who had the number.

"I'm sorry; it seems to be the wrong number."

I dropped off the phone and went out to the street again. I wanted to meet Bob and ask his regards, but I could not. I also did not have a phone of the past. I had enough money to live for months. I worked in prison for seven years. Thanks to it I was able to save some money.

I was able to solve hunger and sleeping for a while because of the money I collected in the prison. Sometimes I went to the shelter and received free food and bedding.

One day I met friendly people and got clothes and necessary necessities. As these lives continue to repeat, I found myself trying to depend on them without my strength. I did not think I would be self-reliant on my own. It was, first of all, to visit Shelter's volunteers if needed. A strong dependency on them began to grow. It began to take its place in me with a habit that can not be easily dispelled.

As the roots grow more and more, the roots of dependence growing in me grew out of me as if they were difficult to pull out from there. These things happened once. I had tried to find a place to work because I thought I should do my job. So, I started looking for a job at the shelter. Within days of starting my job search, I saw an ad that came into my eyes.

It was a company that made toilet paper. It was an advertisement to find the necessary labor immediately. I wrote down the phone number of the company and set the appointment place and time.

I visited the company. I met the interviewer and said I wanted to work there. At that time, his reaction and facial expressions still cannot be forgotten.

He was a man in his early sixties. He was wearing a beard and black horn glasses. He was very intelligent about his age. Perhaps it was the president or executive officer of the company.

For the first time, there was a saying to me.

"Your name is Jim; do you have a criminal background? My company has to be clear, creditworthy, need a trustworthy person, so employees do not have any trouble working."

I could not say anything to his question.

I could not say, 'I've been to a prison for a while because I have a bank robbery career in the past.' I had left the company without saying anything. The miserable heart of that time could not be said.

My regrets about my mistakes in the past have flowed like a tide. At that time, I did not know the result now.

Everything that I misjudged and acted on remained a bad fruit to me. I never thought that these results would be given to me. Since that time, I have not worked and tried to find a job. I did not even try.

Wherever I went, my past criminal career followed me like a shackle. It was like a scarlet letter. Since that day I spent a lot of time on the streets. One day I walked the streets in front of a church. It was the name of the church where I heard it a lot.

The name of the church was the Lutheran. It was the church that Pastor John Rod served. However, some phrases put on the front door of the church. It was a phrase to announce the funeral service.

'Pastor John Rod was called to God as a people of heaven at the age of 90. As a pastor of this church, I will announce the funeral service for the deceased who served for 20 years as the former

senior pastor.
Date: January 20, 2012
Place: Lutheran Church
The charitable donations are donated to poor
neighbors and hospital patients.'

I felt the sadness deep in my heart when I saw the phrase. He was the one who taught me the Bible for the first time. He was the one who inspired faith. After I came out of prison, I did not find him.

But now that he has passed away, I feel sorry for Pastor John Rod. If I knew I would go back to this place, I would have visited at least once and given a greeting. Isn't it next week on January 20? I thought I had to go to see the last of the pastor on that day.

I will leave the world when I will be like him. I did not live like a pastor like him, but I learned from him that it was not bad to live like that. In some ways, the pastor was one who could be called my spiritual father.

Until then, I was not so religious. I did not attend church regularly. I would not have lengthened my homeless life if I were religious and had an independent mind to overcome everything. Until then, I still had a lot of fuss about the world. I went back to the street again. I felt that there was no place for me to welcome me warmly. The streets were as severe as the cold weather.

Life there had to overcome all temptations. Especially, the temptation to get drugs at night was unbelievably strong. There are dealers selling drugs every night. They were young, riding good cars, and all were associated with gangs. They decorated their body with an unknown tattoo.

Most of them were carrying weapons. In the streets, there is frequent controversy among the gangs. Because of their realm, fighting occurs among those who invade the area.

Even shooting occurs and people die. Among the homeless, there are those who related to drug sales that they employ. Instead of selling drugs to others, they get drugs for free.

Most of the homeless on the streets are addicted. Some people take many drugs together and even die. And they are drunk with drugs and sleep in the streets in the cold winter.

Last week, a drug addict fell asleep on the street and died instantly on the spot by a car accident. The temptation to drug here is really lethal. I also had many temptations during my stay in the streets, and sometimes I had been tempted to take drugs. At first, it seemed sweet, but there were many cases of serious side effects that led to increasing addicting and later dying slowly.

There were countless days when I could not eat anything. The money I had already got to the bottom, and I went back to the past days when I had been searching the trash and picking up the bottle and selling it. Every day a horrifying night continued.

I went back into a deep despair swamp. Sometimes it was solitude loneliness by sharing with the shelter or social service organization. My body began to become more and more damaged. Due to drug addiction, the body was not in a healthy.

Everyone looked me older than a middle-aged man. My stomach could not digest the food again, and the body was weakened to the point where it could not be touched by medicine.

I remembered the words of the pastor in the prison. Sometimes Satan is busy and instead sends it to humans, the three of which are drugs, alcohol, and gambling.

I was the one who had experienced all three. My body was almost desperate. There was no difference from the dead.

Chapter 14

MY MEMORY was not as clear as before. Drug addiction is fatal to the human brain. It causes more and more dementia. I did the same. People gave me the advice to go into rehabilitation centers for addicts. But I could not.

I could not resuscitate my body so I could not control myself. Sometimes volunteers came and helped, but they had no effect on the resurgence.

I began to get deeper. I started taking the drug that was the most powerful for a stronger stimulus. However, by the time of the awakening from the drug, more pain and suffering came. I thought of myself as a person dying like this. It seemed to have lived only one meal per day.

It was all lunch that was given in the shelter. All government subsidies received about once a month were taken away by drug dealers. They were really leeches. No one likes them on the streets. They were like vampires who sucked the blood of the poor and the homeless. I have heard that gangs sometimes fight against each other and get shot or caught by the police. Here, no one poured sympathy for what they were doing. I thought it was a punishment.

It was illegal to sell drugs in Canada. But taking drugs is allowed in a legitimate place. So, if people go to a public restroom, they can find someone to use, dispose of their syringes and other related things safely. This was not a safe area for drugs even deep into high school and middle school. All of this was deeply related to the violent gangs. I hated them.

Although I am drowning in a swamp that I can not break out of, I hate gangs. I thought that if they were to disappear from this street, I would solve the drug problem naturally. Those five years of living on the streets with drugs were times I had lived in the dead tombs in my life. My existence in the world was buried.

I went to the burial service of Rev. John Rod, who left the last world.

Many people participated in worship to see the pastor who was leaving last. I stood outside the chapel and witnessed a funeral service so I would not be a burden to others.

Lutheran Church's Gilbert Logan pastor led the worship service.

He was a young pastor and he just seemed to

come to Lutheran church. I quietly closed my eyes and listened to his sermon.

"Today we gather here to send Rev. John Rod, our beloved pastor, to the Lord's bosom, for he was the one who strived to resemble the Lord in his lifetime, always approaching neighbors with smiles and kindness. For thirty years he has preached the gospel for prison inmates and has dedicated himself to the homeless and the poor around us, just as Jesus Christ came to this land and looked back at the weak people. We must follow his ministries, and we must be friends of the poor today, following the will of the pastor who was an advanced believer."

Indeed, it was a sermon that reaches out to the heart. When I was alive, I remembered Pastor John. He did not lose laughter all the time. And he was kind to anyone he met. I thought that someday I would like to change my whole life and go the right way, just like him.

I participated in funeral service and quietly left the chapel as soon as the sermon was over.

It was because there were other people's eyes, and most importantly, I was living below John's expectations.

It was kind of sorry for him. Because I could not keep my promise of swearing with the pastor that I would live a normal life and never do bad things again. It seemed that I lived because I could not keep my life and abandoned it more deeply because the pastor who had the most spiritual dependence left the world. Everyday life was at stake.

It's like a little boat sailing on a sea of storm. I had to endure countless days like darkness.

At that time, I spent more time on survival than in life. When I think about it now, it seemed so stupid at the time. I could have been able to get out of the darkness if I thought a little bit, but as someone was blocking my eyes and ears, my will was frozen and I could not come forward.

"Jim, you have to think that there is always a chance before you wherever you go."

"What is that opportunity?"

I suddenly remembered the words of the pastor.

"You are always ready for a new way to get you off the wrong track and back on the right track."

"Is the road ahead of me?"

"Well, for example, we're driving a car, and then we've lost our way, where we go, one way back to where we came from, But it's already too far away, so we're running out of gas and running out of time."

"Then, Pastor, is there another way we can choose?"

"It's just finding a new way, where there's always a way, and that's where it goes."

"Pastor, is there any way I can go forward?"

"Jim, do not worry, there's a road somewhere, it's your decision, it's your decision to not go back the wrong way."

When I think about where my decision has gone wrong, it seemed like it was a secondary student's day when all of them could graduate and start their social life. I quit school on the way. But I thought that my decision was correct at the time. However, I found myself walking on the road somewhere else. At that time I had to graduate from high school. Even if I had only a minimum number of diplomas, I probably did not choose the wrong path.

But I could not go back to high school at that time. My will was a shattering feeling. No one could stand by me.

After the pastor left the world, I felt that my true commitment to my spiritual dependence had disappeared. I heard a wind blowing through the buildings in the street. The sound resembled a man's cry. When someone walked through the building forests, I was not confident of reaching out to see whether I could reach out and ask for help.

Among the people living on the streets, they had no will to stand up with self-reliant. Most people were always trying to rely on someone. Perhaps if they had intended to be self-reliant, they would not have lived on a cold street.

Their future, which is always exposed to crime, is uneasy. I did the same. I belong to a young age group among homeless people. There were from most of their 40s and to 70s. In society, there were quite a few people who had stable jobs and business. But suddenly it was the streets where people who had no place to go because of unemployment, divorce, or business failure finally chose. They easily fall into the bog of crime or almost abandon themselves because of drug addiction. They always give a lament to themselves. I listen to their stories. An old man always carries photos of his children and grandchildren in his arms.

If he wants to see it, he can not go to it, so he will just be satisfied with the photos in his bosom instead. Sometimes I think about the meaning of the family for them. People in the darkest corners of society respond sensitively to the word family. Most of them think that they have been abandoned by their families. They resent their wives who lived with together for the rest of life and laid hands on the Bible.

And despite their children, they complain

about not finding themselves. And the causes of all the defeat are due to circumstances that are inevitable. So they fall into drugs and gambling to forget that pain. It is the most fragile human figure. They were never strong.

I did the same. Every day repeating pattern made me realize that the street was the most comfortable place and made me adapt to street life. I received a small personal tent from a volunteer organization to stay through the cold winter. It could stop the cold winds, snow, and rain. I was accustomed to the cold, so I was able to endure a winter of Canada in the tent.

Of course, I have been with the homeless people who have been visiting from time to time. I drank every night and fell asleep. Then I could forget the cold to some extent. However, when I woke up late in the morning, I felt pain enough to break my head.

Chapter 15

I STILL could not forget that night. Maybe it was the moment when I entered into a new path of change in my life. That night was the last week of December. Many people were busy preparing for the New Year.

But I did not have anything special to do and I slept all day in the tent. I was so drunk that I could not eat anything, and I slept in the tent in the street.

I heard a voice that someone was calling me outside the tent. I could not tell whether the main character of the voice was a man or a woman.

"Are you in? Can you see me for a moment?"

I barely looked out. There were a middle-aged man and a woman of old age standing there.

"Who are you?"

I slowly asked them in powerless voice.

"The weather is still cold and I'm here to tell you about the dangers of freezing. And I have a few things to tell you."

Kindly they gave me anxious words.

"I can handle the cold. Do you have warm water or coffee?"

"Sure, here is a cup of warm coffee, and your body will be a little warmer."

"Thank you."

I drank a cup of warm coffee they had delivered on the spot. The warmth of the coffee seemed to spread throughout the body. The coffee had a hazelnut flavor. It was my favorite incense.

"But have you been here for a long time?"

"It's been a couple of years now, and I've been roaming Hastings many times before."

"Is there still a lot of people living here on the street?"

"Sure, I think about 300-400 people are probably here, but here's where Hastings lives, and there are a lot of charitable organizations that need it. And so many organizations give me a lot of things. Here's my overcoat I'm wearing from the Salvation Army. It's very warm."

"It looks warm to me."

"Thank you for giving me this coffee, but

what have you come to me for? As you can see, I can not help you anymore."

"No, I do not mean to help me; I just want to invite you."

"Is it an invitation? Did you say you invited me now?"

"Yes, it is an invitation, so we have come to this."

"What kind of charity do you come from?"

"It's very close to here, Lutheran church at the street corner."

I was surprised to hear that Lutheran Church. Lutheran church was where Rev. John Rod was.

"Did you say that Lutheran church? Isn't that the church that Rev. John Rod, who has already passed away, was a pastor?"

"Do you know Rev. John Rod?"

"Yes, I know, he was the first pastor I met at the prison, and he invited me to the Bible study and gave me many good words.

"Yes, it is the will of Lord to meet you."

"Well, rather than the will of the Lord ..."

I felt that it was awkward to say that I meant the Lord. It was because I still had a deep sense of doubt as to whether the Lord would meet me.

"But why did you invite me, do you have any meetings?"

"In fact, we have prepared an event for our

church to invite neighbors this weekend, and we have created a time for a theater to perform, to share the Lord's words with the meal, and to hope that many of you here on Hastings Street will come. Could you come?"

"I want to go there, but my appearance is so poor that I wonder if I can go there?"

"We welcome everyone. Don't feel like any kind of pressure."

"When do you plan to hold the event?"

"We start at 5:00 p.m. tomorrow and hold for three days. You can come and dine and watch the play and listen to the words."

"Then, I will try tomorrow. Thank you for inviting me."

"Don't mention it. May I have your name? If you come tomorrow, please find me. My name is Hamilton, Elder."

"I am Jim, I'll see you tomorrow."

Even if there were only those who came to me like this, life on the street would not be lonely. Maybe I've been waiting for such people every day.

Because I was so weak that I could not stand on my own, I may have been eagerly desperate for someone to raise me up. The loneliest being on earth is probably a human being.

I think and feel. I can not forget those who have come to me when the boundary between

good and evil is already falling down.
After meeting with them, I went back to deep sleep again.

That night, I dreamed. It was a faint spirit that can not distinguish between reality and ideal. I stood on the street. Strangely no one was on the streets. What were visible were the red leaves that had been dripping from the dry branches of the tree and getting wet on the street and stuck on the cold floor.

It seemed as though they were wriggling alive. It looked like the tongue of the street. The streets seemed to tell me something. But I did not know what that sound meant. I stretched out my hands and crawled on the floor. My knee got cold. I tried to stand up, but I could not get up because I felt a strong force holding my back heavy. Everything that stood still felt like living on the streets. I knew then. This street I live in is not dead.

It just felt like my consciousness could not wake up and was dead. I tried to find a person, but the things that passed by me were the wind, the wet leaves and the sidewalks of the streets. Now I had to do something. I could not be lying like this. I eagerly waited for the color of the traffic lights to change from red to green. I had to take the last bus to come to this place in time. My memory began to fade, and I could hear the sound of a chant outside the tent. The sorrow will soon be over. There is always a long tunnel with an entrance and an exit. I am reminiscent of his face while listening to familiar voices. The dawn will come soon.

It was a morning of awakening from a deep sleep and a dream. It was not that cold. The warm morning sun was shining brightly into the tent. Even the headache that I felt every day did not bother me. It was a feeling of clarity. It was the first time I felt like this. I got up straight and went to the nearby shelter.

There, breakfast is provided free of charge. Living on the street I did not have much breakfast any time of the day. But that day I felt hunger. As soon as I opened the shelter door, I greeted the volunteer Philip, who welcomed me in front of the door, in a loud voice.

"Good morning, Philip!"

Philip looked at me and made me look amazing.

"Jim, it's been a long time. How have you been?"

"Philip, I've been good all along, I just did not have breakfast, so I did not have a chance to meet you often, but today I've come to eat breakfast this morning."

"Of course, come on. We always welcome

you."

Philip volunteers mainly in the morning. Already he retires and comes out every day to provide food, cook in the kitchen and clean the shelter. I thought I was ashamed when I saw him. He was already an old age and I was still young, and what I could do was to live in a meaningless life as a loser, drinking and homeless on the streets.

I ate a simple breakfast, seated at the seat that Philip appointed. Bacon and freshly baked bread, coffee and eggs. I felt like I had a good meal in the morning.

After breakfast, I did not just go out of the shelter. I remained there and helped clean the floor and washing dishes. Of course, it was the first time for me. The volunteers came to see me helping with the cleaning work and I also chatted with them.

I was sorry for eating breakfast for free. Something I wanted to do to help them. And after work, I left the shelter and started walking down the street. There is still plenty of time to meet the Lutheran church members. Many people were enjoying a walk out on the street because of the warm weather. A few days later, the New Year is coming.

In their expressions, there was an expectation for the New Year and sadness about the time to leave. When I returned to my tent again, it was already over 12 o'clock. I picked up a small booklet that I picked up on the street long ago in the tent. It was a very thin book with about 150 pages. I thought I would read it someday in the tent, but I could not move it to practice. But thanks to the early rise, I opened the first page with the intention of reading once more. When I read the book's preface, it seemed to be about the basic doctrine of Christianity.

However, it was mainly a questionnaire containing explanations and questions related to our lives, rather than the sermons we hear in traditional churches.

It was not written in a complex language. It was easy for anyone to read and understand easily. I did not go to college. And I stopped at the secondary. I could not continue my studies. So I did not learn much more than others. It was hard to understand when difficult words came out. But this book was different.

Anyone could easily read and understand. I tried to find out who wrote this book. But the author did not mention who wrote the book. It seemed to have been written for those who did not believe in the purpose of preaching the gospel. The book was asking the following questions. It was using the passage from the Old Testament Ecclesiastes.

These are the words of the Teacher. He was the son of David. He was also the king in Jerusalem. "Meaningless! Everything is meaningless!" says the Teacher.
"Everything is completely meaningless! Nothing has any meaning." What do people get for all their work? Why do they work so hard on this earth? Ecclesiastes 1

'Everything Is Meaningless.'

The preface of the book was beginning to do so. Everything in this world is meaningless. At first, I did not know what this meant. Whether he is talking about nihilism or King Solomon, who has everything, is not satisfied with what he has.

If I were King Solomon I would live a satisfying life. He wondered why he had said all things were vanity. So I decided to read a little more. In the book, people say that they do not own everything from birth. Firstborn in empty hands. And even when they die, they return to empty hands. People just go back to the dirt when they die. So whatever it is, it is something that will soon disappear from the world.

No matter how rich the rich are, and even the poor, the place where they will eventually return is the place where the things of the world cannot

150

be taken. So the author of the book says that everything is in vain. I do the same. Of course, I still have nothing, but I always seem to be feeling the lack of something. I couldn't figure out what it was about, but there seemed to be a void somewhere in the deep recesses of the heart. It was a place that was filled with what it was. Even though it was in my body, I could never go there.

+   +   +

I came back to the street again. And I went to Lutheran Church, which I promised them. Thinking deeply about the book I had just read in my mind. I did not want to die when I lived on the streets in my life. A woman who was sleeping drunk on the road near the tent where I stayed a few months ago was hit by a car and died on the spot. Her name was Tony Wood, a woman from Alberta. Perhaps it was a woman who was a prostitute for men.

The one I always remember was to wear heavy makeup and red nail polish. She wore high heels and always stood on the road where I lived. Perhaps she missed a person and found a friend to talk to. People on the streets were quickly erased from people's memories. I did not want to live that life. My grandparents often told me that everyone was born and had a meaning to life. It is said that it means finding its meaning while growing. I also wanted to do that.

I wanted to prove that life is never meaningless or in vain. So today I wanted to go to Lutheran Church with that question.

There was a feeling that I could get the answers that I wanted to go there. The church was not far away. It was a small church that was decorated with old marble. I stepped on the stone steps. On either side of the stairs were beautifully decorated Christmas decorations.

A small sculpture symbolizing the birth of the baby Jesus was also seen. And at the door of the church, there was the phrase, 'Peace of the Lord for all who come in here.' I opened the door and heard a small bell. The church was warm. I waited for a while sitting on a chair in the corner.

And I waited for warmth to warm up. People were busy preparing for various things in the church. Perhaps it was like preparing a meeting for people like me. The chapel had a folding chair and a table.

A while later, a man approached me and talked to me. He was Hamilton, Elder who came to the tent last time.

"Hello, it is nice to meet you once before, I am Hamilton, the elder of this church."

"Hello, I am Jim, thank you for your last

visit and thank you for inviting me to this church event."

The elderly retired long ago, and now he was living a meaningful life, serving the Church. His impression looked gentle.

His impression seemed mild. The first impression was good enough for anyone to approach and talk comfortably. His kind heart might have brought me here.

"Jim, would you like to come over here? I have a seat and a table in the chapel. It would be nice to go there and talk to them."

"Thank you."

I went into the chapel he guided. There were about 10 tables and chairs around them. Many people were sitting there talking. I could see people who live on the same road as me.

"But what are you doing in a church today?"

"Jim, we have time to invite people who are in difficult situations of our neighbors to share the Word and the meal together. You can come to this place every week and listen to the conversation and share the fellowship."

"For what purpose are these people gathered?"

"It is time to pray and learn together about the various problems, beliefs, and lives of your life over the next 10 weeks. People call it the Alpha Course."

"Did you say Alpha Course?"

"Yes, it is an Alpha course, it's a Bible study that started in England, but it's time to learn the truth by applying it to the Bible with the theme that is closest to our lives."

"Do some topics differ?"

"There are many themes, such as God, the Holy Spirit, Jesus Christ, the Church, sin, spiritual struggle, the meaning of life, etc. And we will proceed with counseling. Many people have come here to consult and to be cured."

"Do you counsel drug addicts or alcoholics?"

"Of course, our church has specialists in counseling, and through them, you can get help."

His kind words gave me much comfort. Maybe then I might have been waiting for somebody's help. While living on the streets, I could not escape from hell by strong powers that I could not know. Drinking and drugs made me crazy. I wanted to get out of the way, but I was already a captive of darkness.

I decided to attend the Bible study offered by the church steadily. The talking subject was 'What was the theme of that day was life?' It was in line with the theme of the book I read in the tent before I came to church. It was not a coincidence. The pastor of the church came out as a leading pastor. And he gave me the words of Ecclesiastes which I had read.

"I am glad to meet you, I am John A. Ashley, the pastor of this church, and I welcome you sincerely, and the theme we want to share today is the Ecclesiastes, Our life is vanity. We live without any purpose, why we are born in this world and how we should live, and where we should go if we die. I'd like to ask you a question. Are you happy with your life right now?"

I could not answer his question. It was because I had lived so far without any purpose. Of course, I am not happy now. In his question, the people gathered there were silent.

"It's a question that can not be answered easily, but one thing is clear: even though we have got what we want, it is easy to feel thirsty again as if we are hungry again. We are spiritual beings, and that is the difference between animals. Mental and physical things can be somewhat satisfying. But the spiritual part is not filled, so we are always sad and unsatisfied. The Bible clearly says the Lord will be the true object of worship and God is the true shepherd and guide that fill our spiritual problems."

I felt deep sympathy for saying that life is meaningless. And I did not know why. But here I came to know the reason. Yes, I was a spiritual being. Because I was not filled with spiritual parts in me, I was always looking dissatisfied when looking at life. I have seen a lot of people who commit suicide themselves.

Especially among the homeless. They had something in common. Everyone said that life is pointless. I did not know the meaning at first. But now I think I can find out a little bit. It was because they did not realize that they were a spiritual being. Our indigenous people were very spiritual people. I have now come to realize why my ancestors made so many statues and shamanic beliefs. It was because they wanted to solve spiritual things.

But they wanted to solve spiritual problems in things that exist in nature. But the pastor said that we must go to God to solve our spiritual problems. The ancestor's found objects from nature, but the pastor said that they should seek from God. For nature is nothing but his creation. Because God created us, the purpose of our worship is God.

It was a moment when I realized what the purpose of my life was. It was the time that the question which always heavily burdened was solved. My steps to go out of the church were light. It seemed to me that the unforgettable joy was felt from my deep inside. I have not missed a week since then and attended church meetings. I did not experience any strong miracles or mysterious things, but I began to feel myself walking into the Word. The world was truly amazing. The world of the Word was like the sea. I was like a little child who had ever played in shallow waters. I was a man who lived without knowing the secrets of the deep sea.

A great change in my life began to come. By the end of the last two months, I decided to go find my pastor. The reason was to abandon the way of life so far and to continue the impression and determination that I realized in the meeting. I thought it would be pointless if it ended only as a meeting and there was no change. The first thing I need to do is find someone now and ask him for help. I thought the pastor was the right man. Through the pastor, I became acquainted with the deep world of the Word.

Before I visited the pastor, I repeatedly read down the phrases that were deeply moved by the words I studied. I unfolded the Bible from the church and remembered it in my heart to find the underlined word. I recited if necessary.

There was a power to heal the heart of a person so that I could wield the word. It was as though the letter could live like this. How the letters written 2000years ago could move people's mind today.

I could understand that the Word was sweet as honey. On Sunday, I began to participate in worship. I sat in the corner of the back seat of the chapel, listening to the Word and singing praises so as not to bother others. By the end of the Sunday afternoon worship service that day, I went to the office where a pastor was. The office where the pastor was located was at the end of the corridor behind the chapel.

The pastor was at rest at the end of Sunday sermon.

"Pastor, its Jim. Can I come in for a while?"

"Of course, come on in. Have you been good all along?"

"I've been good all along, and it was an unforgettable time for me."

"How was the church Bible study meeting?"

"It was so impressive, and I have had time to look back on myself as I have lived."

"It is good news to hear that you have come to realize many things through those times, Jim, Jesus loves you now, and now you are inviting you to hold on to the Lord. You must hold the Lord's hand. You need to make a decision to overcome and live a new life, and that time has come to Jim. We will help you."

"Thank you, Pastor, what shall I do?"

"First of all, let me make Jim work in our church, you need an income from the job, of course, we will pay you, you will be an employee of the church, you know that our church is running a shelter. We built shelters for the needy and the homeless. We need a person to work there, I hope that Jim will do the work, I will arrange a room where you can eat and sleep, and I hope to continue your Christian life in the church. You must overcome with the power of faith. We will pray for Jim."

The pastor's suggestion for me was very grateful. I suddenly thought Pastor John Rod who was passed away. When I was in prison, the pastor always worried about me. And it came to his mind that he was praying. At that time, I did not know the pastor's heart.

I have come to realize that perhaps it was Reverend Rod's prayer that was able to get me out of the deep quagmire of despair. I can not forget now the feeling of walking down the street from the minister's office. I felt like I was getting lighter. Everything looked warm. Everything looked warm. The sky was warm and the rain was wet on my face, and everyone around me felt warm.

+   +   +

Now I know that there is something I need to do someday even if I start the day. It was just a series of meaningless lives last day. It was a miracle to me that I, who had been on drugs late at night and had lost consciousness and had slept on the streets, now had a desire to free myself from the pain and live like others. Every changed day was thanks to me. It was as if the young child came out to visit the outside world for the first time in mother's womb, and was curious about the curiosity of the new world. I moved all my stuff to the shelter.

All things were old clothes and a few books. I heard from my predecessor what I had to do and I started my work. Since I first dropped out of high school and worked at Tim Horton, I got my job. Of course, at that time, I did not go to church. But now the situation is different. As I had faith, I became confident that I could live a normal life like everyone else. I decided not only to help the homeless but also to work hard for my own future.

To get a high school diploma once again, I applied for a credit acquisition program for adults online. If I get a high school diploma, I want to get a technical education. If I have a little dream, I will learn baking skills and become a bakery shop boss. So I wanted to help people like me. And I want to live for a mission as a volunteer in the church.

For the poor neighbors and for the natives of the land like me. Some time I went to my friend Bob who I met at the shelter for the first time. Yet he did not have faith but wanted to let him know what I experienced when he needed it. He has recovered a lot and now he has been able to talk with me often and to share fellowship.

I hope to visit him often and help him. Our lives are not that hard. As always, after the rain, we must know that our lives are so changed and time is waiting for us to experience new things, just as the earth is firm, the sunlight meets the beautiful rainbow.

I was not alone when I was born. People always watching and cheering me ran with me from the beginning. I would like to dedicate this article to all of them.

-End-

ABOUT THE AUTHOR

Yongjea John Han majored in Law and English Literature, majoring in theology in the Netherlands and the United States. He also worked as a poet in Korea. He then moved to Canada to continue his work as a writer and missionary. He and his wife and two children, near Chilliwack, BC, are dedicated to a mission for the weak and writing activities. This book is his first novel.

[Books: *Slow City, The Space, Refugees, The Old Memories of Tynehead, The Qs about AIists, Refugees Ali, Jesus On the side of the Weak, Epistles from the drifters 1, Wetland City, The Living Breath, Theology for the Weak, The Covenants of God*]